The Beauty
of
Holiness

Nelson S. Perdue

Unless otherwise noted, all Scripture is from the
New King James Version—NKJV

Whispering Pines Publishing
11013 Country Pines Road
Shoals, IN 47581

ISBN: 978-1-934447-66-6

The Table of Contents

Preface 5

1. Holiness: The Central Principle of Creation . . . 9

2. Holiness: The Central Principle of Redemption . 12

3. The Promised Gift of the Holy Spirit 20

4. Vessel unto Honor 28

5. The Pure in Heart 35

6. Perfecting Holiness 43

7. Spiritual Liberty 49

8. Pentecost: The Consequence of Calvary 55

9. The More Excellent Way 65

10. The Inheritance of the Saints 73

11. Sanctify Them 79

12. Jesus: The Lamb of God 88

13. Holiness: Its Beauty and Mystery 96

Preface

The Psalmist cried, *"Let the beauty of the Lord our God be upon us"* (Psalms 90:17).

He admonishes, *"Give unto the Lord the glory due unto His name; Bring an offering and come before Him. Oh, worship the Lord in the beauty of holiness!"* (I Chronicles 16:29, Psalms 29:2). Beauty is not only a great incentive to holiness; it is its essential essence. There is nothing more beautiful than holiness, nothing more desirous than purity, and nothing more abiding than love. This characterizes the life of the Spirit-filled Christian and enables him to adorn the doctrine of God our Savior in all things. Holiness is always beautiful when perfect love flows from a pure heart and these are the qualities of entire sanctification.

Arch Bishop William Temple defined worship as:

The submission of all of our nature to God. It is the quickening of the conscience by His holiness, the nourishment of the mind by His truth, purifying the imagination by His beauty, opening of the heart to His love, and the submission of our will to His purposes. And all of this gathered up in adoration is the greatest of human expression of which we are capable.

Sanctification partakes of the divine nature in the sense that iron partakes of the fire; the rough, rude iron put in the fire becomes radiant, brilliant, and the fire may say to it: "I have imparted that to thee." So God may say to the soul, "I impart to thee the glow and beauty and warmth of my nature; thy soul is bathed in God."

We know that it takes all the primary colors of the spectrum coalescing to make pure white; so it takes the various attributes of holiness joined together, coalescing, to produce the pure white light of the beauty of holiness. The beauty of holiness includes the beauty of: purity, harmony, devotion, humility, love, Christ-likeness, and perfection. It is God's command: *"Be holy, for I am holy"* (I Peter 1:16). When the child of God experiences the joy of all past sins being forgiven, he realizes not only that he is a debtor to his Savior, but there is a love that yearns only to be pleasing to the one to whom he owes his forgiveness. The Holy Spirit soon makes him aware of a need that forgiveness did not meet. He discovers a perversion in the depths of his moral nature that cries for deliverance. When he hears the beckoning call to make a complete and living sacrifice of himself to his Savior, he immediately hungers and thirsts for righteousness. The call to holiness to him is not a dread, but a delight. He soon realizes that the epochal work of entire sanctification is not only essential, but is most desirous because it brings about spiritual health and harmony. He graciously makes a complete consecration of himself to his Savior. He, then, by the hand of faith, is able to reach into the sacred death of the Son and appropriate the provisions of full salvation made available on Calvary.

It has been my happy privilege to proclaim this truth these past forty years. Holiness begins in regeneration, made perfect in entire sanctification, and will one day be consummated in glorification. When one is sanctified wholly, he has laid the foundation upon which to build the superstructure of his spiritual life that will stretch all the way to heaven. Although sanctification is instantaneously obtained, it is ever capable of improvement, development, and progression.

The Sainted Fletcher said:

Filled with all the fullness of God describes a state of grace far beyond entire sanctification. We enter the sanctified experience from the negative hemisphere, realizing the utter elimination of the sin principle through the cleansing blood. Having past the sin side of the experience, we enter the glorious hemisphere of abounding grace which is illimitable in this life and superseded by the glory of heaven, sweeps on in a geometrical ratio through all eternity, ever and anon flooding the soul with fruitions, amplifications, beautifications, and rhapsodies eclipsing the

6

most ecstatic hyperboles, while ages and cycles wheel their precipitate flight.

If this little volume shall be the means in the hands of God of helping some soul who is crying for a clean heart into its full enjoyment, we will give all the glory to Him whose blood cleanses from all sin. I pray, under the direction of the Holy Spirit, it proves to be a blessing to everyone that reads it.

1

Holiness: The Central Principle of Creation

When one considers the God of creation, he recognizes that He is infinite in every attribute of His being. He is infinite in His knowledge, wisdom, power, justice, and righteousness. However, the essential attribute of God is holiness. It has been stated:

> Holiness is the very God of God. Holiness is necessary to His existence as God. God's blessedness is in His holiness. It constitutes the heaven of His infinite being. God is independently holy. No one has been His counselor, and no one has been His sanctifier. He is holy in and of Himself from eternity.[1]

> Because He is holy, He is just.
> Because He is holy, He is love.
> Because He is holy, He is merciful.
> Because He is holy, He is truth.
> Because He is holy, He is light.

His glory is the outshining of His holiness and is unmixed goodness. His holiness is absolute, infinite, and non-forfeitable. Because He is holy in His character, He is holy in His works. He always acts consistently with His nature, so there is never a margin between what He is and what He does. He is, therefore, as free from mistakes as He is free from sin.

Holiness is the eternal and unchanging standard of God. The time came when God decided to create man, the crown of all creation. It was then that the triune God-head entered the counsel

---

1   J. Paul Taylor, *Holiness, The Finished Foundation*

chambers of eternity, and consultation was held and a decision was reached that God's own holiness would be the prototype of man's original state. Man became the expression of His own infinite perfections. The holiness of God involves the perfect moral balance of the total of all He is. Glory being the outshining of His holiness, God proceeded to create a race of moral beings capable of sharing His glory. In His high priestly prayer in John 17:22, Jesus prays *"and the glory which you gave me I have given them, that they may be one."* It is holiness alone that qualifies man for His glorious presence. Holiness, therefore, is the central principle in the act of man's creation.

Man was clothed in glory and placed in a pristine paradise called Eden. The mind can only imagine the beauty of this garden. Everything was conducive for man's pleasure and enjoyment. That measure of beauty, harmony, peace, and blessedness in such an environment will never be known again until we are welcomed into the place God has prepared for His children. This was all possible only because God, who is holy, created man a holy creature and placed him in a holy place called Eden. Holiness was the central principle in the place of man's origin.

A free moral being must be possessed with the power to do either good or evil. However, having the power to do a thing neither necessitates our doing it or makes it right for us to do it. While man was created with the power to do wrong, he does not have the right to do wrong. Why God made man with the capacity to sin has been a problem for many to understand. Capacity itself is unmoral, it is the use that a free being makes of capacity which gives it quality, either moral or immoral. Man is a divinely created moral and responsible being with a capacity for God and holiness and with a capacity for evil and unholiness. God loved man whom He created and endowed him with the capacity to love in return. It is the nature of love to desire to be loved, and so He desired that man would willingly reciprocate love. Love to be true to its nature cannot be coerced or forced. If He gave him the capacity to freely and willingly love Him, that fact naturally carries with it that man would also have the capacity to reject Him. As long as man loved and obeyed the cre-

10

ator, all was joyful bliss. Holiness always manifests itself in love. Holiness was the central principle of the Garden of Eden.

It needs to be noted that before God released His energies that brought about man's creation, He provided for his redemption if it became necessary. Before man's fall in the Garden, God had already planned, if needed, the provisions for man's redemption and restoration. In Revelation 13:8 we are told about *"the Lamb slain from the foundation of the world."* Again we read, *"Just as He chose us in Him before the foundation of the world, that we should be holy and without blame before Him in love"* (Ephesians 1:3). It has been stated that there was a cross in the heart of God before there was ever a tree from which to make one. Long before man ever needed a Savior, one was provided for him in the counsel chambers of eternity.

Man created in the image and likeness of God was holy. Apparently there would be a time of probation or testing in order for the moral choice of our first parents to conform to the perfect will of God. If man would have obeyed the will and word of God, the character which they possessed would probably, by their own free will, have become a fixed state of character. The tragedy is that man disobeyed God and was banished from the holy place called Eden. *"He placed cherubim at the east of the garden of Eden, and a flaming sword which turned every way, to guard the way to the tree of life"* (Genesis 3:24). In so doing, he prevented man from taking of the tree of life and becoming forever fixed in his sin. He is now able, if man will respond to His call, to redeem and once again restore him to that image that sin has effaced.

Sin came about because man's selfish will rebelled against the highest authority of the universe. Self-will is the very central image of the devil, while the central image of God that was forfeited is, *"not my will but thy will be done."* Man now finds that he is no longer God-centered, but self-centered. God immediately initiates the great plan of redemption to restore the image of God in man.

11

2

Holiness: The Central Principle of Redemption

Man was made for God and His glory. With glory being the out-shining of His holiness, unholy man cannot share in His glory. Man is potentially a son of God. Grace proposes to restore him to his potentiality through the efficacy of the Cross. The holiness which Jesus provides in the Redemptive plan is in quality like God's own holiness. It is, however, bestowed upon man and inwrought for him as an earthen vessel. It is the same in quality as in God, but it is modified by human limitations. Unlike God, there is a margin between what a man is and what he does. His motive may be pure, but often-times his methods of doing are flawed due to the infirmities and ignorance of the earthen vessel. Therein is the difference between evangelical Christian perfection and absolute perfection. One may be correct in his motive, and yet because of limitations and human infirmities may fail in judgment and conduct. Such failures and mistakes are entirely compatible with a holy heart. *"For the Lord does not see as man sees; for man looks at the outward appearance, but the Lord looks at the heart"* (I Samuel 16:7). However, because the true believer wants to be pleasing to his heavenly Father and be an example of faith to the world around him, it is incumbent that he is careful in all of his conduct in order to walk worthy of the calling to which he is called.

Immediately following man's disobedience, God put His plan of redemption into motion. In Genesis 3:15 we see its early intro-duction when God said to the serpent, *"I will put enmity between you and the woman, and between your seed and her Seed; He shall bruise your head, and you shall bruise His heel."* Here we see God taking the battlefield to redeem, restore, and reclaim His own.

John tells us that God was active in creation, through His Son. *"In the beginning was the Word, and the Word was with God, and the Word was God. He was in the beginning with God. All things were made by Him, and without Him nothing was made that was made"* (John 1:1-3). The Apostle Paul says, *"For by Him all things were created that are in heaven and that are on earth, visible and invisible, whether thrones or dominions or principalities or powers. All things were created through Him and for Him. And He is before all things, and in Him all things consist"* (Colossians 1:16-17).

He was also active in human redemption for the *"Word* (who was the creator) *became flesh and dwelt among us, and we beheld His glory, the glory of the only begotten of the Father, full of grace and truth"* (John 1:14). The writer of Hebrews tells us in the first few verses of his letter, *"God who at various times and in various ways spoke in times past to the fathers by the prophets, has in these last days spoken to us by His Son..."* God had something to say to us that no poet or prophet could say, and He spoke through the Incarnate Word. Through His life, death and resurrection, our Lord has made complete provision for the full moral recovery of man. The supreme objective of redemption is given in God's command recorded in I Peter 1:15, *"But as He who has called you is holy, you also be holy in all your conduct, because it is written, be ye holy, for I am holy."* It is this standard that constitutes the complete moral recovery of man.

As from the beginning in creation, holiness was the supreme and essential requirement of man's likeness to his Creator God, so it is the supreme and essential requirement in redemption. If holiness of heart and life is the most essential truth of Christianity, then the true value of everything else within the redemptive scheme must be measured by its relation to that which is most essential. The value of our ministry, whether it is through our teaching, preaching, witnessing, or any other means of grace is dependent on our ability to produce, promote, and propagate experiential holiness in all of its stages.

Let us examine God's great plan of salvation and look at the various and sequential requirements necessary to restore him back to God's righteous standard. Holiness is not only the central theme of the Bible but the supreme objective of redemption. From Genesis to Revelation, holiness is paramount. The Word of God is constantly revealing to us the purpose of the passion of Christ, *"To grant us that we, being delivered from the hand of our enemies, might serve Him without fear, in holiness and righteousness before Him all the days of our life"* (Luke 1:74-75). Here we see that if we fully dedicate our lives to Him that He will fully deliver us from all sin, and the duration is **"all the days of our life."**

Because of the fall of Adam, sin has alienated the human race from God. *"Therefore, just as through one man sin entered the world, and death through sin, and thus death spread to all men, because all sinned"* (Romans 5:12). Paul tells us that natural man is, *"dead in trespasses and sins, in which you once walked according to the course of this world, according to the prince of the power of the air, the spirit who now works in the sons of disobedience, among whom also we all once conducted ourselves in the lusts of our flesh, fulfilling the desires of the flesh and of the mind, and were by nature children of wrath, just as the others.... BUT GOD, who is rich in mercy, because of His great love with which He loved us, even when we were dead in trespasses, made us alive together with Christ (by grace you have been saved), and raised us up together, and made us sit together in the heavenly places in Christ Jesus, that in the ages to come He might show the exceeding riches of His grace in His kindness toward us in Christ Jesus"* (Ephesians 2:1-7).

Here we see that through the atonement, Christ has provided for us a way of escape from Satan, sin, and our own selfishness to put us on the highway of holiness that leads back to God. There are conditions necessary for us to meet in order to appropriate the provisions of Calvary. We are not left to ourselves to struggle to meet these requirements, for He is there to assist us all the way. Jesus tells us that *"no man comes to the Father except through me"* (John 14:6). He further tells us that *"he desires all men to be saved and come to the knowledge of the truth"* (I Timothy 2:4). Let us look at what this great plan of salvation requires of us and let us, unlike Adam, be instant in our obedience to His command. *"For if by the one man's offense*

(Adam) *death reigned through the one, much more those who receive abundance of grace and of the gift of righteousness will reign in life through the One, Jesus Christ"* (Romans 5:17).

Sequential Steps to Holiness:

Jesus promised His followers before He ascended back to the Father that He would not leave them orphans, but that He would send the Holy Spirit to them. The Holy Spirit would administer all that Christ had provided in His death and resurrection. He would guide them into all truth, teach, and comfort them. Jesus also told them that *"when the Holy Spirit has come, He will convict the world of sin, and of righteousness, and of judgment"* (John 16:8). Without the drawing conviction of the Holy Spirit, man would never find his way back to God. It is the Holy Spirit that convinces the sinner that he is lost and needs a Savior. He is the one who persuades him to repent and believe that he might be saved by grace. He employs various means to bring the sinner to the realization of his need. He uses the providences of life, the prayers of Christian people, the preaching of the Word of God, but in the final analysis, He is the one who persuades the sinner to repent. Having repented, he now stands forgiven of all past sins and justified before God his Savior. He has found this new life in Christ.

As he walks in the light, he will soon recognize a problem that forgiveness was not able to meet. He will be convicted of a need that only the cleansing blood can meet. The Holy Spirit is revealing to him the remains of sin that lurks in the heart. It is the inbred sin that the human race inherited because of the fall in the garden. One is not responsible for it being there, but since its discovery, he is responsible to seek its cleansing. He is called upon to make a complete consecration to His Savior. He is now able to identify with the crucifixion of Christ in a most intimate way. He, like Paul, can say, *"I have been crucified with Christ; it is no longer I who live, but Christ lives in me; and the life which I now live in the flesh I live by the faith of the Son of God, who loved me and gave Himself for me"* (Galatians 2:20).

15

The steps of faith: conviction, repentance, consecration, and crucifixion are necessary and sequential. By sequential, I mean that one cannot occur without the previous one. One must first be convicted, followed by repentance, without which one cannot make a complete consecration, followed by an inner crucifixion where the child of God can declare that he is *"dead indeed unto sin but alive unto God."* The true value of every step is measured by its relation to the most essential part of the redemptive scheme. Every step in the process is a step in holiness. When one is entirely sanctified, he has laid the capstone on the foundation upon which he now may build upward forever.

Holiness not only has its relevance in this world, but also in the world to come. One must also acknowledge its perpetuity and its permanency. **In the past**, following man's creation and previous to his fall, sin was not a part of his world and life, but holiness was the central factor and principle of his being. The standard of Holiness existed in principle in the Garden of Eden before any part of the plan of redemption was ever needed or necessary. **In the present**, because of the fall of man, God's plan of salvation has required that man meet certain and sundry conditions in order for him to, *"put on the new man which was created according to God, in true righteousness and holiness"* (Ephesians 4:24). However, the various facets and conditions of salvation are only means to an end. Even in this world, holiness of heart and life exceeds all other experiences of the soul. **In the future**, holiness will be the only part of God's great plan of salvation that will be carried beyond the grave. There will be no more need of conviction, confession, contrition, repentance, forgiveness, consecration, crucifixion, and such like, but *"without holiness no one will see the Lord"* (Hebrews 12:14).

The primary purpose of the church, through our witness, testimonies, praying, teaching, and preaching is to bring everyone into this hallowed relationship. The Apostle Paul in (Colossians 1:28-29) says, *"We preach, warning every man and teaching every man in all wisdom, that we may present every man perfect in Christ Jesus. To this end I also labor, striving according to His working which works in me mightily."*

16

John Wesley said, "And wherever the work of sanctification increased, the whole work of God increased in all its branches."[2]
In a letter to Mr. Merryweather, February 8, 1766, he said:

Where Christian perfection is not strongly and explicitly preached, there is seldom any remarkable blessing from God; and, consequently, little addition to the Society, and little life in the members of it....Till you press the believers to expect full salvation now, you must not look for any revival.[3]

John Wesley further insisted that Christ died for man's sanctifying, as well as justifying, that God's processes include a second definite work of grace, and that love is the universal evidence of one's inward holiness. "Our main doctrines," he said, "are repentance, faith, and holiness. The first of these we account, as it were, the porch of religion; the next, the door; the third, religion itself."

Holiness is the greatest theme of the scriptures. It is the foundation of the nature and character of God and of saints and angels. No one can be a true Bible preacher without preaching holiness. The Bible begins with a holy pair in a holy Garden and ends with a holy church in a holy city. All the way in between is holiness. The deeper the church dwells in True Holiness the more successful she is in her God-given purpose.

God gave the commission to *"go into all the world and preach the Gospel to every creature. He who believes and is baptized will be saved; but he who does not believe will be condemned"* (Mark 16:15-6). We might just as well believe that the sinner will be saved without the preaching of repentance as to expect that the believer will be sanctified wholly without the preaching of second blessing holiness. We must be as specific in preaching entire sanctification to the believer as we are to preach repentance to the sinner. We, as Christ's Church, must be faithful to declare the central principle of redemption in order for man to be fully restored to his lost estate. This is her primary purpose; everything else is secondary.

---

2   *Works of John Wesley, XIII*, 350
3   *Works of John Wesley, XII*, 270

17

One stated:

If Social Activities crowd out this purpose, we become nothing more than a religious lodge.

If Government Usurps this purpose, we are prone to become a religious political machine.

If Education Encroaches we are apt to become a system of intellectual elitists.

If Entertainment is too strongly emphasized, we will be reduced to an emotional religious center.

But if she retains her primary purpose of declaring the Whole Counsel of God and leads men and women into a state of full salvation, she'll remain a gateway to heaven for hungry hearts. The deeper she dwells in holiness, the more successful she will be in her God-called purpose. Concerning the Church of which Christ is the head, let me quote some distinguishing beliefs, summarized by one of her chosen sons, Dr. Gideon B. Williamson:

1. We believe the Bible as God's Word is the foundation for our Faith and the Rule of our Living.
2. We believe that all men are lost who are without Christ as Savior.
3. We believe that Jesus died to save and sanctify wholly all who believe.
4. These beliefs provide sufficient cause for all-out evangelism to convert the world and lead all men on the way of holiness to heaven.

We must believe that what we preach is a life or death issue. We must have a new appreciation for our distinguishing beliefs as well as a new dedication to them. Those who would dilute our doctrines, discount our experiences, compromise our standards, and divert us from our purpose are the most effective agents of our destruction. They make it easy for themselves and others to take the broad way. We are in a vulnerable position when our lines of demarcation are dim. It is time to renew our covenant with God, our forefathers, and our posterity.

We Are "Called to Holiness!"

It was stated earlier that every step in the plan of redemption is a step in holiness. Perhaps it also should be stated that every step is a process in salvation. We often hear it said that some sermons are salvation sermons, and some are holiness sermons, as though a message on holiness or sanctification is a message on something other than salvation.

The word "**salvation**" is a very comprehensive term. When the sinner repents and is converted to the faith of Christ, we say that person received salvation. He did indeed; in fact, you may speak of it as *free salvation*. However, when a believer is sanctified wholly, he experiences *full salvation*. When the day comes and one finishes the race and receives the crown of life, he will experience *final salvation*. Free salvation saves us from our own sins (transgressions); full salvation saves us from (inbred or innate) sin; final salvation will save us from the scars and presence of sin. The reason I make this distinction is to remind us that sanctification is a salvation blessing as much as the new birth. The Apostle Paul tells us, *"But we are bound to give thanks to God for you, brethren* (born-again ones) *beloved by the Lord, because God from the beginning chose you to salvation* (heaven) *through sanctification by the spirit* (entire sanctification) *and belief in the truth"* (II Thessalonians 2:13).

In the following pages of this book it is my purpose to develop some Biblical expositions with special emphasis on the second work of grace. In so doing, I'd like to reveal its relationship to the first work of grace, disclose its importance as necessary equipment for the work to which He has called us in this life, and also show that it is preparatory for the life to come. The call to holiness is not optional; it is essential; it is not discretionary, but imperative.

19

3

The Promised Gift of the Holy Spirit
(Acts 18:24-19:7)

This passage of scripture begins by introducing us to a man by the name of Apollos. He was born in Alexandria, Egypt, and he came to Palestine. Through the ministry of John the Baptist, he was converted and baptized. He was a man that was very well educated, eloquent, and mighty in the Scriptures. "He knew only the baptism of John. **Bengel** says: "He had the Spirit, but not in that special way that is treated in Chapter 19:6, but in the ordinary way."

The New Testament scholar, **Alford** says, "He was instructed in the things of Jesus," but as yet having only experienced the baptism of John. There was no question that he had been regenerated because John did not baptize anyone who did not give evidence of their repentance.

Daniel Steele says of Apollos:

He was acquainted with all the facts of Christ's earthly life, Christian baptism included, but had failed to see that while John's baptism symbolized the negative side of sanctification, the putting away of sin, or death to sin, Christian baptism prefigures the positive part, the fullness of the Divine Life through the baptism of the Holy Ghost. ... The great defect of Apollos, therefore, was in not having a correct view of the extent of Gospel salvation through the baptism and indwelling of the Holy Spirit in the office of the Comforter and Sanctifier, and in the absence of the experience of this Spirit-baptism. ... He had not experienced that distinct and specific Pentecost—the crowning work of Jesus as foreseen by John, *"He shall baptize you with the Holy Ghost and fire."*

John Fletcher says:

The ordinary work of the Spirit is like the dew; the extra ordinary is the outpouring of a mighty shower. Apollos had been moistened by the dew, but not drenched by the shower."[4] He was like many Christians today; while he lived in the Pentecost Age, he had a pre-Pentecost experience. In other words, he had received the baptism of repentance which John administered, but had not yet received the baptism with the Holy Ghost that only Jesus could administer.

We are told, *"When Aquilla and Priscilla heard him, they took him aside and explained to him the way of God more accurately"* (KJV *'more perfectly'*) (Acts 18:26). When I read this account, I am struck with two thoughts. **The first** thought is what were Aquilla and Priscilla able to detect listening to him that convinced them that he had something lacking in his faith? They certainly had a spiritual discernment.

I'm reminded of the two ladies who prayed for D. L. Moody that he would be Spirit-filled. Though a mighty man of God, they knew something was lacking, and they sought the Lord on his behalf until he was filled with the Holy Spirit, and it made his ministry far more effective. He later testified when asked, "Does D. L. Moody have a monopoly on the Holy Spirit?" His response was, "No, but the Holy Spirit has a monopoly on D. L. Moody."

The second thing that I was impressed with was the readiness of Apollos to listen and respond to their advice. Aquilla and Priscilla were very devout laymen who were wholly sanctified while associated with Paul in tent-making and the work of evangelism while in Corinth. Apollos was a very educated, brilliant, and eloquent man, yet he was very humble and teachable. He could have said to these laymen, "Why would you, who are unlearned, try to instruct me concerning anything?" He, no doubt, saw in them a depth of love and humility and spiritual sensitivity that was lacking in his own heart and life.

---

4   Daniel Steele, *Milestone Papers* pg. 138-139.

This leads us into Chapter 19 where the Apostle Paul comes into Ephesus and meets up with twelve disciples and asks them the question, *"Did you receive the Holy Spirit* **when** *(*KJV *since) you believed? So they said to him, we have not so much as heard whether there is a Holy Spirit"* (Acts 19:2). Later in Verse 6 it is recorded that *"when Paul had laid hands on them, the Holy Spirit came upon them."*

It is important to note that all Christians have the Holy Spirit. Paul in (Romans 8:9) says, *"If anyone does not have the Spirit of Christ, he is not His."* He further states in (Galatians 4:6), *"And because you are sons, God hath sent forth the Spirit of His Son into your hearts, crying out, 'Abba, Father'!"* When Paul asks, ***"Did you receive the Holy Spirit when you believed?"*** He was not speaking of a different Holy Spirit; it was not the difference in His Person or Personality, but the difference in His relationship and capacity. He is the same Person, but with a deeper relationship.

I have had young couples greet me, and the man would introduce his lady as his fiancé. I have met the same couple months later, and the gentleman would introduce his lady to me as his wife. She is the same lady, but in a much different and more intimate relationship.

Paul was asking these disciples if they had received the Holy Spirit (not in the fullness of His Personality), but in the fullness of His operation. They had known the Holy Spirit as one who reproved them of their sins and regenerated their soul. They knew Him as Savior, but not yet as Sanctifier. They, like all God's children, needed to know Him in the glorious gift of His fullness.

Jesus prayed for His children before He went to the cross that they would receive the Holy Spirit. He promised that He would send Him to them. In Acts 1:4-5, Jesus admonished His disciples: *"Wait for the promise of the Father, which, He said, you have heard of me; for John truly baptized with water, but ye shall be baptized with the Holy Spirit not many days from now."* This promise came to fulfillment on the Day of Pentecost. It was the same promise recorded in (John 7:37-39), which says that when Jesus was glorified, He would send the gift of the Holy Spirit.

The Reception

The question Paul posed to these disciples in Ephesus and is relevant for us today, is not have you done, or given, or joined, or been sprinkled, poured, or immersed but, "**Have you received?**" Salvation is a gift at every stage of the spiritual life whether it is our pardon, purity, power, or our preservation. It is not something we grow into, but something we receive. It is not something we have done, but a gift to be received. It is not by our own grit, but by God's grace. It is not an accumulation of what we already have, but an investment of what we are to receive.

The commission that the Lord gave to Paul was that he was to go to the Gentiles, *"to open their eyes, in order to turn them from darkness to light, and from the power of Satan to God, that they may receive forgiveness of sins and an inheritance among those who are sanctified by faith in me"* (Acts 26:18).

The whole plan of redemption is on the basis of a gift. God gave His Son; Christ gave Himself, and the Holy Spirit gives gifts. One must be impressed when he sees how lavishly God pours out good gifts to man. He is also made aware that one cannot be a Christian in the likeness of His Savior if he is not a giver to his fellowman. When we receive, then we are privileged to give. *"For everyone to whom much is given, from him much will be required"* (Luke 12:48). When one receives the Holy Spirit, Jesus says, *"out of his heart will flow rivers of living water"* (John 7:38).

The Reason

Paul knew that these twelve disciples were neither ready nor equipped to accomplish God's will in Ephesus if they were not filled with the Holy Spirit, just as Jesus knew the disciples would be powerless unless and until they waited for the promised Holy Spirit to purify and empower them on the Day of Pentecost. The Apostle recognized the urgency of this matter, knowing they, too, would be powerless without His purifying presence empowering them for service.

23

The Methodist missionary, Dr. E. Stanley Jones said that following this incident, a revival began that lasted three years and three months. He said that it shook Ephesus from its center to its circumference even spreading on out into Asia Minor. Several churches were started and thousands of dollars worth of bad literature was destroyed. One can only imagine what God could accomplish today if all of God's children would rise to claim their birthright and be filled with the Holy Spirit.

The baptism with the Holy Spirit that John the Baptist said only Jesus had the "worth" and "might" to perform in the heart of his children, is essential to salvation. It expiates the sin principle from the believer's heart and enables one to fulfill God's call on his life. It is a salvation blessing (an indispensable part of it) and when one receives light on the experience and conviction for its need, it is imperative that they respond immediately and obediently to the call to holiness. *"God from the beginning* **chose you for salvation through sanctification by the Spirit** *and belief in the truth"* (II Thessalonians 2:13). Paul warns that, *"He who rejects this does not reject man, but God, who has also given us the Holy Spirit"* (I Thessalonians 4:8).

Many Christians have never received or experienced this second work of grace in their heart. In light of this scripture, I want to offer a possible reason as to why that is true. Perhaps they have never heard that the Holy Spirit is given to them in this capacity. (We are unlike these twelve disciples who had not yet heard that the Holy Spirit had come into the world following the ascension of Christ. We know that He is now in the world. This is the Holy Spirit's dispensation. Many have experienced the birth of the Spirit, but perhaps they are not aware that they are now candidates for the baptism of the Spirit. In the birth of the Spirit one enters into life (free from guilt of past sins), but it is through the baptism of the Spirit that one is emancipated in life (set free from inbred sin).

Paul says, *"How then shall they call on Him in whom they have not believed? And how shall they believe in Him of whom they have not heard? And how shall they hear without a preacher?"*... *"So then faith comes by hearing and hearing by the word of God"*

24

(Romans 10:14, 17). He further states in (Colossians 1:28), *"Him we preach, warning every man and teaching every man in all wisdom, that we may present every man perfect in Christ Jesus."* Perhaps one reason why many have not experienced the baptism with the Holy Spirit as a second work of grace is because it is not being preached or taught. If that is the case, then it is an indictment against the ministry because we have failed in our call to proclaim the whole counsel of God.

When God commissioned His disciples to go into all the world and preach the Gospel to every creature, He meant the "**whole**" Gospel. He said that when the Holy Spirit (Comforter) would come, He would guide us into "ALL" truth. It is no more irrational to suppose that the heathen (sinner) might be evangelized without the preaching of the Gospel, than to suppose that the believer might be sanctified wholly without the preaching of holiness. False teachers are not only dangerous for the errors and heresy they espouse, sometimes the danger lies in the truth they omit.

Requirements

There are conditions that need to be met in order for the believer to experience entire sanctification, a work that is the effect of the baptism with the Holy Spirit. Salvation in any and all of its stages is contingent upon one walking in the light. As has been stated previously, the central image of God in man is not **self-will** but rather **His will** be done in us. We know that in I Thessalonians 4:3, 7 Paul says, *"For this is the will of God, your sanctification...For God did not call us to uncleanness, but in holiness. Therefore he who rejects this does not reject man, but God, who has also given us His Holy Spirit."*

Oswald Chambers warned,

Beware of saying, I am longing to be sanctified wholly; if God has not sanctified you wholly and made you blameless, there is only one reason. and that is because you don't want Him to. This is the will of God, and you do not have to urge Him to do it.

25

The obvious condition required to be a candidate for this experience is one must be **unworldly**. Jesus says, *"The Spirit of truth, whom the world cannot receive, because it neither sees Him nor knows Him; but you* (believer) *know Him, for He dwells with you and will be in you. I will not leave you orphans; I will come to you"* (John 14:17-18).

Obedience is another condition to receive the fullness of the Holy Spirit. In other words, we must be walking in all the light and not living in a strained relationship with Him. We must be in a loving, obedient relationship without any reservation in our consecration and willing to resign all in total abandonment to Him.

It has been stated that consecration is one simply returning stolen property. Indeed Satan, sin and self robbed our heavenly Father of man, the acme of creation. He owns all rights on us, and we were meant to be His beloved possession. He loves us so much that when sin separated man from his God, God was willing to come into the world and offer Himself as the sacrificial Lamb and pay a high price to redeem and ransom him. Therefore, when we give ourselves to Him, we must not use our consecration as a purchase price for the Holy Spirit. We must not try to drive a hard bargain as if to say, "If I give my all to God, what can I expect from Him?" That is an insult to a loving Father.

We are instructed to **ask** for the Holy Spirit. Jesus says, *"If you being evil, know how to give good gifts to your children, how much more will your heavenly Father give the Holy Spirit to those who ask Him"* (Luke 11:13). The Holy Spirit is the Father's love gift to His children. Conviction for entire sanctification demands a clear consciousness of our need and faith that Christ will fully satisfy the need of the soul. No one ever entered into the experience of entire sanctification who felt that he could get along very well without the experience.

The **Faith** for entire sanctification (the Promised Gift of the Holy Spirit) is strengthened by the three words found in Luke 11:13, *"How much more."* To illustrate the phrase, one might ask, "How much more does the light of the noonday sun exceed the light of a candle?" and realize there is no comparison. *"Now to Him who is* *able to do exceedingly abundantly above all that we ask or think, according to the power that works in us"* (Ephesians 3:20).

This experience of entire sanctification is as distinct from the new birth, the first work of grace, as rivers overflowing are distinct from wells springing up from within. The question Paul asked the twelve believers in Ephesus, *"Did you receive the Holy Spirit when you believed?"* must be answered in the affirmative by all who truly love Him and want to live a life pleasing to their Lord.

4

Vessel unto Honor
(II Timothy 2:14-21)

The Apostle Paul is coming to the end of his ministry and life on this earth. He gives his dying testimony in Chapter four and states that the time of his departure from this world is at hand. Before he leaves he gives some last minute instructions and admonitions to Timothy, his young son in the ministry. He brought to his remembrance the rich Christian heritage that had been passed down to him. He reminded him that the genuine faith that was in him was due, in large part, to the faithfulness of his grandmother Lois and his mother Eunice.

He instructs him concerning the devotion and discipline of the Christian walk. He knew that he would face trials and dangers that would challenge his faith, and he encouraged him not to despair, for *"God has not given us the spirit of fear, but of power and of love and of a sound mind"* (II Timothy 1:7). He wanted him to be true to the doctrines of the Gospel and not be ashamed of him who was imprisoned for the defense of the faith. There would always be heretics spreading their heresy, and for this reason he encourages him to *"Hold fast the pattern of sound words which you have heard from me, in faith and love which are in Christ Jesus"* (II Timothy 1:13).

The Apostle Paul was a devout Jew who, following his experience on the road to Damascus, was sent to deliver this Gospel to the Gentiles. He faced ridicule and persecution from his countrymen, and now about to be beheaded he says, *"I am already being poured out as a drink offering."* He had no fear because he said in (Philippians 1:21, 23), that death to him would be gain and that his desire was to depart and be with Christ. He also left this testimony

"I know whom I have believed and am persuaded that He is able to keep what I have committed to Him until that day" (II Timothy 1:12). He knew **"Someone"** (Christ) not a mere **"somewhat,"** and was willing to suffer the loss of everything to see Him face to face.

Paul was drawing a picture of the church for Timothy. He speaks of its foundation, structure, and its besetting dangers. He points out that there are many who claim to be a member of His church who have not truly been converted. They may know the historic Christ, but they do not know Him as their Redeemer. These heretics have come with their heresy teaching that the resurrection is already past, and they were trying to destroy the hope of many. They sought to bring injury to the house and harm to its occupancy. He assures Timothy to be steadfast in the faith because these heretics cannot shake or shatter the church's sure foundation.

In speaking of the solid foundation of His church, he declares two things that seal it both in its character and its destiny. The first is the recognition by God of all those who are His own. He said, *"I am the Good Shepherd, and know my sheep, and am known of mine"* (John 10:14). The second seal is the renunciation of all that is evil by those who name Christ as their Savior. This speaks of the structure of this great house. Let us now look at the occupancy of the house.

Paul speaks of two sorts of vessels in the house, some for honor and some for dishonor. It is possible that the word dishonor refers to those who pervert the truth such as Hymenaeus and Philetus who had strayed concerning the truth. He makes plain that if we are going to serve as honorable vessels in the house of God we must be obedient to the call of God who loved the church and gave Himself for it and be true to its doctrines. The Apostle reminds us that *"He saved us and called us with a holy calling"* (II Timothy 1:9). This calling is subsequent to the saving because the call is not extended to the sinner, but to the saved. It is a call to the Christian to be sanctified. Robertson says that the saved is "called to a life of consecration." We believe that the call to holiness means more than consecration, although it certainly involves it. Whatever is consecrated must be purified and made morally clean by the God to whom it now belongs.

The sinner is concerned primarily with getting rid of the guilt of his sins. It is only after he becomes a child of God and is enjoying holy aspirations and desires that he recognizes a conflicting spirit. Along with holy desires he begins to feel the presence of a sinful nature within that hinders him from living a holy life. It is then that he seeks cleansing from the carnal mind. *"Therefore if anyone cleanses himself from the latter, (Purge himself from these KJV) he will be a vessel for honor, sanctified and useful for the Master, prepared for every good work"* (II Timothy2:21).

Purified

It is necessary for one to cleanse or purge himself from all things that would defile. This defilement may have reference to the vessels of dishonor which is represented by evil companions. It also would include any evil passion or moral perversion which exists in the soul that seeks gratification. Separation from all defilement is an essential part and condition of sanctification. Entire sanctification has two sides to it, the human side and the divine side. Separation and consecration is man's part of entire sanctification, and actual cleansing is God's part. Man separates himself from all that would defile him and consecrates all that he is and has to God.

This law of purgation is mentioned in many places and by several of the New Testament writers. John, in his first epistle speaking to the sons of God who are anticipating the day of hope when Christ appears, says to them, *"Everyone who has this hope in Him purifies himself, just as He is pure"* (I John 3:3). Peter is speaking to the believers who are followers of good, that they should *"Sanctify the Lord God in your heart"* (I Peter 3:15a). In this sacred act the finite heart becomes the habitation of the infinite God. It is the crowning of Christ as Lord of our lives. This is when He establishes His reign in our hearts, and He always cleanses (sanctifies) the temple of His dwelling. In his letter to the Corinthians, Paul reminds us that we are the temple of the living God. *"Therefore come out from among them and be separate, says the Lord. Do not touch what is unclean, and I will receive you. I will be a Father to you, and you shall be my sons and daughters, says the almighty."* Having just addressed the children of God, he further instructs them. *"Therefore, having these promises, beloved, let us cleanse ourselves from all filthiness of the flesh and spirit, perfecting holiness in the fear of God."* (II Corinthians 6:16-7:1)

We, in the human act of consecration, cannot **actually** cleanse ourselves, but **conditionally** and **cooperatively**, we can and we must. We cannot sanctify ourselves, but God cannot sanctify us without ourselves. It is only when we make a complete consecration of ourselves that we are then able, by faith, to appropriate the cleansing blood. This faith by which we are made holy is a moral act, and while it is aided by the Holy Spirit, it is so essential that, without it, God is powerless to cleanse us. When one exercises faith, God affirms to that obedient heart, *"You have purified your souls in obeying the truth through the Spirit"* (I Peter 1:22).[5]

God will never bestow His honor on an unholy people, but only on those who are His holy ones. If we want His smile of approval on our lives, and if we want to experience His pleasure, we must eliminate any and all perversion and immorality. It is only then that we will receive His seal on our lives, for *"the Lord knows those who are His."* This is the solid foundation of God that is steadfast and sure. No one who rejects the call to holiness will receive His endorsement.

Qualified

The word "Sanctify" is the verb that speaks of cleansing and when one is sanctified wholly he then becomes the honorable vessel that is useful to God and His kingdom. Their value is greater than wood and clay. He now is fully fashioned and fitted for the service that God has called him to perform. While holiness is essential for the world to come, it is the necessary qualification to do the work and will of God here and now because purity of heart is practical for holy living in this world. It is not only the wedding garment for the world to come; it is the working garment for this world.

5   Paul S. Rees, Sermon: "Let Us Be Clean," 1936 *Pilgrim Holiness Advocate*

He now is *"prepared for every good work."* It is the sanctified that God uses to pour Himself through. John tells us that *"He who believes in me, as the scripture has said, out of his heart will flow rivers of water."* He spoke concerning the Holy Spirit. (John 7:38-39a) This experience enables one to live, love, and labor to the glory of God, for he is *"prepared for every good work."* No matter how menial the task would seem to be, every pure heart does a good work. One may not be called to lead, but all are called to love out of a pure heart. While the world cannot see Christ within us, they certainly will recognize the Christian conduct reflected in our walk and work.

Peter, speaking in Acts 15, said that God showed no favors to the Jews when it came to purifying their hearts because He purified the hearts of the Gentiles as well, and it was through faith that the work was accomplished. This truth shows that sanctification is a crisis experience. It is not an instinctive process after conversion. One does not grow **into** holiness from something else, but once they, by faith, enter into the experience they will grow **in** holiness.

John Wesley taught clearly that sanctification is both instantaneous and gradual. In 1767 he wrote, "I believe this perfection is always wrought in the soul by a simple act of faith, consequently, in an instant. But I believe there is a gradual work, both preceding and following that instant."

The life that follows demands constant vigilance and discipline. Timothy says, *"Flee also youthful lusts; but pursue righteousness, faith, love, peace with those who call on the Lord out of a pure heart. But avoid foolish and ignorant disputes, knowing that they generate strife. And a servant of the Lord must not quarrel but be gentle to all, able to teach, patient in humility, correcting those who are in opposition, if God perhaps will grant them repentance, so that they may know the truth, and that they may come to their senses and escape the snare of the devil, having been taken captive by him to do his will"* (II Timothy 2:22-26). Christ has given to us the ministry of reconciliation, and as His ambassadors, God is pleading to the sinner through His Spirit-filled children. This is the vocation to which He has called us.

Sanitized

Isaiah 52:11 says, *"Be ye clean that bear the vessels of the Lord."* When one studies God's directives concerning the ceremonial cleansings in Leviticus and elsewhere in the Old Testament, he is struck with the importance that God places on purity and cleanliness. These were types and shadows of a deeper moral cleansing that He provided for us on the cross. In the verses that head this chapter, it is quite evident that if we are going to be profitable for the Master's use we must be clean vessels. This is not only necessary for us to be fit for His use and for us to find freedom from all moral defilement, it is also a protection for those to whom we minister. Let me give a physical illustration to clarify a spiritual truth.

When one enters a hospital with a physical malady that requires surgery for its healing, we expect that the doctors will use clean surgical tools and use them with clean hands. Everything is scrubbed clean for fear that staph infection will occur and cause injury and even death.

If sanitation and sterilization is so important when ministering to the physical needs of a person, how much more important it is when ministering to their spiritual needs. Jesus knew that His disciples were not ready to minister to the world around them immediately after His resurrection. That is why Jesus commanded His disciples to wait for the Holy Spirit to come upon them on the Day of Pentecost. It was then that they were purified from all sin and empowered to be witnesses in Jerusalem, Judea, Samaria, and unto the whole world. If they had not waited, they, like a doctor with unclean hands and tools, would have inflicted great harm not only on themselves, but also to those to whom they were called to minister.

As the vessels of God we must keep in mind that entire sanctification is not automation. One is not sanctified once and for all, but rather by maintaining a constant and complete consecration it is once and for always. Even Jesus, when He prayed in His High Priestly prayer in John 17 *"I sanctify myself,"* was giving to us an insight into sanctification. He had and was not only a holy Self, but it was this holy Self that He denied all the time. It was deprived of sleep, comfort, food, possessions, and eventually His life. It was His holy Self that Satan tempted to disobey the Father. We must keep in mind that the servant is not greater than His Master. Away with the idea that once we are sanctified wholly that we can do as we please. The sinless Son of God lived a life of self-denial and in Romans 15:3 it says, *"For even Jesus did not please Himself."* When we are identified with our Lord in sanctification, it is then that we begin to understand the real meaning of the cross. Paul writes, *"God forbid that I should boast except in the cross of our Lord Jesus Christ, by whom the world has been crucified to me, and I to the world"* (Galatians 6:14).

May our prayer be, *"**Refining fire, go through my heart;**
*   **Illuminate my soul;**
*   **Scatter thy life through every part,**
*   **And sanctify the whole."***

5

The Pure in Heart
(Matthew 5:8)

The Sermon on the Mount is one of the longest discourses of our Savior recorded in the Bible. This masterful sermon has been called the Constitution of the Kingdom or the Charter of the Church. There are some who say that this sermon is not applicable for this age of grace, but is meant for some future millennial state. They say it is a nice standard for one to approximate, but it can never be fully realized at this time.

However, Jesus proclaimed it while here on the earth in the flesh. He sealed it with the blood of the cross and ascended to the right hand of the Father and sent the promised Holy Spirit. The Holy Spirit would be the power of its performance and the secret of its realization in the lives of His redeemed children.

To live in this very corrupt world with a pure heart is a high standard. It was Dugan Clarke who said of this standard, "It is not too idealistic to be realized, but it is too realistic to be idealized." It would be an impossible standard to live without His indwelling. We are only able to live this sermon in everyday life because the preacher of this sermon lives within us. That is one of the unique aspects of the Christian faith. Every other religion may have some good and honorable teachings, but to live by their teachings is not contingent on the teacher, for he/she is no longer living. Jesus did not merely teach us how to live, but the risen Christ sent the Holy Spirit to indwell His children, and it is His presence within that enables us to live according to His teachings. The Christian's life becomes the out-living of His indwelling; not as a puppeteer manipulating us, but a loving and cooperative mutuality in operation. He works in and through each of His children, and each one maintains their own individuality and personality.

The Christian cannot adopt a few principles of Christianity and try to live them out in everyday life without reference to the person of Christ Himself. They cannot embrace the principles and enjoy the privileges of Christianity without experiencing the person of Christ in their hearts. The Holy Spirit desires to clothe Himself with the believer as He did with Gideon in Judges 6:34 which says, *"The Spirit of the Lord came upon* (clothed Himself with) *Gideon."* However, He will not come into our hearts and cohabit with sin. He comes to gain our permission and co-operation so that He can purify our hearts and make our body the temple of His dwelling.

Heart

The word "heart" is used over 800 times in the Bible and probably 160 of those times it is recorded in the New Testament. When we read this word in the Bible, we must not think of it as the physical muscle in the chest cavity that pumps the blood through the veins of the body to keep us physically alive. However, as that healthy, physical muscle is vital to our physical well-being, so a healthy, spiritual heart is vital to our spiritual well-being. When speaking of the heart in spiritual terms, we mean that it is the seat of the affections, the inner life, the "real" you. It is spoken of in the Bible as having various capacities. Let me list a few of them.

In Genesis 6:5 it says, *"Then the Lord saw that the wickedness of man was great in the earth, and that every intent of the **thoughts** of his heart was only evil continually."* Here we see that the heart has the capacity to think.

In Daniel 1:8 it says, *"But Daniel **purposed** in his heart that he would not defile himself with the portion of the king's delicacies, nor with the wine which he drank; therefore he requested of the chief of the eunuchs that he might not defile himself."* Here we see that the heart has the capacity to **act and make decisions.**

The Bible speaks of a **"bitter"** heart in Ezekiel 27:31.

In Proverbs 14:13 it speaks of a "**sorrowful**" heart.

In Romans 2:5 the Apostle speaks of a "**hard and impenitent**" heart.

In Romans 10:10 the Apostle says, *"For with the heart one **believes** unto righteousness, and with the mouth confession is made unto salvation."*

In Psalms 24:3-4 the Psalmist asks, *"Who may ascend into the hill of the Lord? Or who may stand in His holy place?"* He answers and says, *"He who has clean hands and a **pure heart**."*

James in the New Testament admonishes us: *"Cleanse your hands, you sinners; and **purify your hearts**, you double-minded."*

Paul in I Timothy 1:5 says, *"Now the purpose of the commandment is love from a **pure heart**, and from a good conscience, and from sincere faith."*

In response to a question from the inquiring lawyer who asked, "Teacher, which is the greatest commandment in the law?" Jesus said, *"You shall **love the Lord** your God with all your heart, with all your soul, and with all your mind."*

These and many more of the Scriptures teach us that the heart has the capacity to do a great many things. It is clear that if we are going to be able to perform pleasing to our Savior, we must have a healthy heart. What health is to the body, and what sanity is to the mind, holiness is to man's soul. God has made provisions through the sacrifice of His Son for man to have a "pure heart" and be able to live a righteous life in this present world. Only a pure heart is a healthy heart.

Polluted Heart

Because of man's fall in the Garden, sin has polluted the human race at its federal head (Adam), and this pollution has been passed on to all of his posterity. The heart of the entire human race has been contaminated with sin and has left him unable, in his natural state, to live a righteous life and to love God with all of his heart. Jesus came into the world and was willing to go to the cross and be the "sin offering" that was necessary to salvage, out of the wreckage of the fall, a people who will be a credit to the sacrifice He made. On Calvary's cross He has made provisions for the cleansing of man's heart from "ALL" sin, so he can once again *love God with all of his heart.*"

One must have a Biblical understanding of the nature and extent of sin in order to grasp the nature and extent of God's gracious plan of salvation. The nature of sin is twofold. It is not only a deliberate act of disobedience; it is a disease that has polluted man's heart and is a perversion in his soul. This pollution within man's heart gives him a natural inclination and proclivity to sin. The atonement has provided not only for the forgiveness of man's disobedience, but also cleansing from depravity in his heart.

Notice first what is called **actual sins**: Disobedience to God's law is a willful act because man intelligently consents to it by his own will, and in so doing, he brings guilt upon himself. All have willfully sinned as Paul tells us in Romans 3:23, *"For all have sinned and fall short of the glory of God."* This fact places all men in a common category of demerit and all men under the sentence of death and all in need of a Savior. When man willfully transgresses the law of God, the law of Divine justice condemns him because it acts on the presumption that he could have avoided it.

If man could not refuse to sin (unable to say no to sin) man could not be justly condemned for sinning. However, man is not a machine; he is a responsible moral being. He has the power of choice and free will, and God has made him the arbiter of his own actions. Therefore, one must repent of his sins, and by faith, receive God's forgiveness.

Let us now look at the **state or disease of sin**: The state of sin is not dependent on our will. We can neither create it nor destroy it by our own will. The state of sin is still resident even in the nature of the justified. In justification the state of sin, often referred to as, "**the old man**," is repressed, but in the work and experience of entire sanctification, it is destroyed. The state of sin does not fall under the operation of pardoning grace because it is not something we have done, but that which the human race has inherited from the Fall. A nature cannot be forgiven; it must be cleansed.

In Mark 7:20-23 Jesus reveals the ugliness of an impure heart when He says, *"What comes out of a man, that defiles a man. For from within, out of the heart of men, proceed evil thoughts, adulteries, fornications, murders, thefts, covetousness, wickedness, deceit, lewdness, an evil eye, blasphemy, pride, foolishness. All these evil things come from within and defile a man."* This is a condition in the moral nature of man that the first work of grace, namely pardon, is not designed to reach. It needs to be remembered that the same lips that taught that one must have a "pure heart" reveals that there is such a thing as a "polluted heart." He would not reveal such a state of impurity without providing for its remedy. This He did at Calvary when He died to save man from "ALL" sin, its disobedience and its defilement.

Justification resolves man's sinful-habit life and gives him grace to keep him from continuing in sin. He is so far saved as to not commit sins. Sanctification resolves man's sinful-self life and enables him to love God with all of his heart. It was Wesley who said that God **quickens the dead**, but He heals the **morally sick**.

There are those who teach that deliverance from all sin is impossible while we are yet in the flesh; He will give us power to repress sin. They believe that the human body is inherently evil, and only death will free us from all sin. However, Jesus had a human body and was the sinless Son of God and was our example. *"Christ also suffered for us, leaving us an example, that you should follow His steps: Who committed no sin, nor was deceit found in His mouth"* (I Peter 2:21-22). He never considered the human body evil; in fact, He created humanity and declared it to be *"very good"* (Genesis 1:31).

Repression or suppression of sin does not change the nature of sin any more than a prison cell changes a prisoner's heart. Dr. Daniel Steele writes, "Repressive power is nowhere ascribed to the blood of Christ, but rather purgative efficacy. It is eradication, extinction of being, destruction." He then poses the question, "If the

Holy Spirit cannot eradicate original sin now, through faith in the blood of Jesus, what assurance have we that He can ever entirely sanctify our souls."[6]

It is in this second work of grace that God, through the efficacy of His blood, purifies this deeper area of man's moral nature. Because the pure heart is an essential part of man's salvation and the supreme purpose of redemption's plan, its neglect is dangerous, and its refusal is sinful.

Pure Heart

When we speak of a pure heart we are not speaking of perfection of the intellect, but the purity of intention. When one is justified freely and sanctified wholly, we are not speaking of finality, but fitness; not a perfect head, but a pure heart. There must be a continuation beyond the crisis.

The purity of heart is the negative aspect of the holy life. There is more to heart purity than the absence of sin, just as light is more than the absence of darkness. It is cleansing for the sake of communion and effective service. Peter in Acts 15:8-9 comparing the conversions of the Gentiles with the Jews said, *"So God, who knows the heart, acknowledged them by giving them the Holy Spirit, just as He did to us,* (on the Day of Pentecost) *and made no distinction between us and them, purifying their hearts by faith."* Without this cleansing they were unfit for communion and incapacitated for service. We need a pure heart to enjoy His sweet fellowship and continued cleansing from sin by His precious blood to enable us to fulfill His will on earth. As Tennyson said, "My strength is the strength of ten, because my heart is pure."

Richard S. Taylor says that in Psalms 51:10, David prayed that God would, *"Create in me a clean heart, O God, and renew a steadfast* (right KJV) *spirit within me."* He states, "The word, create is *bara*, a radical word used for bringing into being something previously nonexistent. David begs for more than patchwork or repair;

---

6 Daniel Steele, *Milestone Papers* pgs. 94, 97

he wants a pure inner nature—something he has never had before. Nor is this regeneration—making spiritually alive. It is entire sanctification—making every whit whole." Dr. Taylor further said, "Peter went right to the heart of Pentecost by showing that Pentecost goes right to the heart."[7]

This act of God's creation also produces a "right" spirit—a devout, obedient, believing attitude. When David prayed, *"renew a right spirit within me,"* he wanted to mark the end of the instability that is brought about by the remains of carnality in the heart. He wanted the rest of the soul that only a pure heart would bring, and by faith he laid hold of the promise of a pure heart. It is not something he achieved by self-effort; it was something he appropriated through Christ by a self-surrendering faith. Such is the responsibility of all Christians to experience a pure heart.

Again I quote,

A man may scourge his back and starve his body and live in solitude, and yet not be pure in thought and in heart. But, let us hasten to add, he may, if he will, fall upon his knees and, yielding himself in unreserved devotement to the will of the Almighty Father, cry out in the earnestness of his longing spirit, *"create in me a clean heart, O God."* And He who created the heavens and the earth, who one day will create the new heavens and the new earth wherein dwelleth righteousness, who creates the new life of the spirit in the mystical hour of the new birth, even the God and Father of our Lord Jesus Christ will, by His Holy Spirit, baptize that man with the fire of purification and enable him to live a clean life, full of gracious ministries of love, in the very thick of a wicked world's traffic in sin.

Along with all the benefits of a pure heart, there is also a vital factor of moral safety in the teaching of entire sanctification. While one is never in this world beyond the possibility of sin, a pure heart certainly reduces the possibility of it. When the heart is pure it is an undivided heart. No divided heart is either

---

7   Richard S. Taylor, Sermon entitled: "An Anguished Prayer for Radical Cleansing."

safe or strong. Its security and its utility are together contingent in a very vital sense, upon its singleness of moral quality, and its unity of spiritual purpose and passion.[8]

Most importantly is the privilege of one day seeing our Savior face to face and hearing His words of welcome as we enter into the joys of our Lord. *"Blessed are the pure in heart, for they shall see God"* (Matthew 5:8).

---

8   Dr. Paul S. Rees, Sermon, "The Benediction of a Pure Heart."

6

Perfecting Holiness
(II Corinthians 7:1).

This verse probably should have been the last verse in Chapter 6 rather than the opening verse of Chapter 7 as it maintains a continuity of thought emanating from the closing verses of the previous chapter. In order to give this verse clarity of thought, let us look at the verses just prior to this admonition.

The writer uses the word "therefore" as an index finger pointing back to the conditions that the Apostle lays out in order for one to be a child of God. The appeal in this verse is based on the logic of divine purposes and divine pledges. Let us review the conditions necessary to be able to fulfill the command of our text.

The Promises

The promises of God are always conditioned on man's obedience. In giving man a free will, He desires man's cooperation to establish a loving relationship between Himself and man upon whom He desires to lavish His love. It must, however, be remembered that the fact man has been given a free will; there lies the possibility that this free will could be used against Him instead of for Him and with Him.

It has been stated that, "God sovereignly chose to limit His own sovereignty by granting to the human creature a limited sovereignty. *"I have set before you life and death, blessing and cursing; therefore choose life"* (Deuteronomy 30:19). **"Choose life"**—there is man's sovereignty. **"I have set"**—there is God's sovereignty, self-limited by the option He has given to man." Frederick Shannon says, "God hangs the stars and spins the planets without regard for anyone's belief or unbelief, cooperation or non-cooperation, but He hangs the human destiny on the invisible hinge of the human will."[9]

There are five promises that God gives to those who will obediently meet the conditions required. He promises to dwell in them, walk with them, be their God, receive them, and be a Father to them. In order for these promises to be realized in our hearts and lives, let us examine the conditions He requires of us. Let it also be understood that these are not mere arbitrary requirements to satisfy the whim of a dictatorial despot, but they are necessary in order for a holy God to fellowship with man and to fully satisfy man's capacity for God.

Holiness cannot fellowship with any ungodliness. "It is His holiness that makes Him the proper object of worship. Worship being the highest exercise of which man is capable, man therefore needs an object of worship so high, so absolutely perfect, that his self-abandonment and adoration will result in his continued uplift and betterment."[10]

Holiness is a life of separation. *"Do not be unequally yoked together with unbelievers. For what fellowship has righteousness with lawlessness? And what communion has light with darkness? And what accord has Christ with Belial? Or what part has a believer with an unbeliever? And what agreement has the temple of God with idols? For you are the temple of the living God"* (II Corinthians 6:14-16). He declares the contradistinction in each verse, righteousness and unrighteousness—light and darkness—believer and unbeliever—Christ and Belial, and shows they cannot exist together. Therefore, we must choose whom we will serve. If we are going to be His children, we must renounce our devilish patrimony in order for Him to adopt us into His family. Once we have met all the requirements and become the children of God, we must listen and respond to the appeal of my text. This appeal is given to only His children.

---

9   Paul S. Rees, Article in *The Church Herald and Holiness Banner*, January 9, 1975
10   C. W. Butler, *Faith Building Messages*, Pg. 6

44

The Purity

Dr. Daniel Steele says, "The *aorist indicative* in the Greek language expresses a momentary occurrence of an action in past time, such as, *"I wrote."* The *"present"* tense denotes what is now going on, and indicates a continuous, repeated, or habitual action, such as *"I am writing."* Therefore my text is written this way; "Let us **cleanse** (*aorist tense*, a moment, a crisis). ourselves from all filthiness of flesh and spirit, **perfecting** (*present tense*, ongoing action) holiness in the fear of God.

Cleansing is here viewed as a human work, inasmuch as our application of the purifying power is by faith. The teaching of this passage is that the faith that appropriates the Sanctifier is a momentary act, lifting the soul out of all outward or carnal, and all inward or spiritual, sin. Had the process of sanctification been like washing a mud statue, a continuous and never completed work, as some teach, Paul would not have failed to express this idea by using the *present tense."* [11]

In this appeal by the Apostle Paul, he is saying that while they had been brought into the high relationship as sons and daughters, they who now were enjoying the fact that they had been saved, adopted, regenerated, justified, and all that implies, these experiences had not of themselves conferred a complete moral cleansing. Therefore he appeals to them to *"cleanse yourselves from all filthiness of flesh and spirit."*

Sanctification has two sides to it, man's side and God's side. Man must consecrate fully in order for God to sanctify wholly. It requires man's subjugation in order for the divine operation. Man must fully yield his will in order for God to bestow the fire of His cleansing.

As was stated in a previous chapter:

> ***Actually*** man cannot cleanse himself, but **conditionally, responsibly,** and **cooperatively** he can and he must. In other words, we cannot sanctify ourselves, but God cannot sanctify

---

11   Daniel Steele, *Milestone Papers,* Pgs. 57-58

us without ourselves. In salvation God acts **with**—**not apart** from us, we supply the man, and He supplies the grace. This is accomplished by faith in the blood of the Lamb. *"You have purified your souls in obeying the truth through the Spirit"* (I Peter 1:22). This is illustrated in Revelation 19:7, *"Let us be glad and rejoice and give Him glory, for the marriage of the Lamb has come, and His wife has made herself ready."* Her readiness was not her own achievement for it was truly by grace.[12]

The two things that are noteworthy are: 1. The **entireness of this cleansing**, *"from ALL filthiness of the flesh and the spirit.* 2. **The immediate and decisiveness**, the word "cleanse" calls for a crisis act which is definite and decisive.

The Perfecting

The question naturally arises, "How do you perfect that which is already perfect; namely, holiness?" There can be no increase in purity. A thing is either pure or impure. The word "cleanse" in my text is in the aorist tense, which denotes that it is an instantaneous act. Let us now look at the phrase, "Perfecting holiness in the fear of God." It means to carry into practice.

If holiness is enjoined on the basis of sonship—and enjoyed by us on the basis of faith—it is to be exemplified on the basis of practice. A holiness that will not meet the practical test is spurious. Paul says in Philippians 2:12-16, *'Work out your own salvation with fear and trembling; for it is God who works in you both to will and to do His good pleasure. Do all things without complaining and disputing, that ye may become blameless and harmless, children of God without fault in the midst of a crooked and perverse generation, among whom you shine as lights in the world; holding forth the word of life.'* … This is carrying holiness into practice. [13]

While there is no increase in purity, there may be an eternal increase in love, and in all the fruits of the Spirit. After

---

12 Paul S. Rees, Sermon "Let us be Clean" in the 1936 *Pilgrim Holiness Advocate*.
13 Ibid.

cleansing, our ceaseless prayerful effort must be to gain more knowledge, be more virtuous, deeper sanctity, and every other form of spiritual excellence. This is what is implied by *'perfecting holiness in the fear of God.'* The word, *'perfecting'* is defined in Baxter's Greek Testament Lexicon thus: 'to carry into practice, to realize,' which means that the perfect inward cleansing instantaneously wrought by the Holy Spirit is to be constantly and progressively carried outward into all the acts of daily life. As knowledge increases and conscience is cultivated, there will be quickened sensibilities and more accurate perceptions of duty, which will lead to constant increase of moral beauty and all the fruits of righteousness, until we "stand perfect and complete in all the will of God." [14]

The words *"cleansing"* and *"perfecting"* clearly teach holiness both as a gift and process, both instantaneous and gradual. Not that sin is cleansed gradually, but *"perfecting holiness in the fear of God"* is the progressive side of sanctification.

The sense of the word, *"perfecting,"* is completing, finishing, and carrying forward to maturity that work that has already begun. The idea is that of the garden which has been cleansed from weeds and planted with seeds, and now it is being carried forward to the fullness of the blossom and the fruit. Do not, therefore, let us settle down in self-complacency because we have received the baptism of the Holy Spirit and entered upon a deeper life, but let us go deeper and press farther on until we reach "the fullness of the stature of Christ." [15]

This describes the ongoing action that belongs to the human in total cooperation and consecration to His Lord. It will require prayerful reading of the Word of God and earnest heed to His teachings. There will be the times of apologies and confessions of faults. It will demand humility when one faces rebuke. It matters little who gives the reproof, as far as their character is concerned, for the question should not be, "Who is he or she? or "What is he or she?" but, "Is it true?"

---

14 Thomas Cook, *New Testament Holiness*, Pg 36
15 A. B. Simpson, *Second Corinthians*, Pg. 81

As one walks in the light and enjoys sweet communion with the Savior, His blood will continue to keep us clean. This will prepare and enable him to face any trial or persecution that he will undoubtedly encounter. God does not promise the Christian exemption from these, but He will give us His enabling grace to sustain us and oftentimes provide a way of escape. Peter reminds us that, *"the genuineness* (trial KJV) *of your faith, being much more precious than of gold that perisheth, though it be tested by fire"* (I Peter 1:7). The Apostle Paul suffered as few have ever suffered, yet he declared that all his persecution worked for him *"a far more exceeding and eternal weight of glory"* (II Corinthians 4:17).

While the inward work "cleanse yourselves" is His possibility, the outward work "perfecting holiness" is our responsibility. There is an after-work following the altar-work. Though one is cleansed from all sin, the aftermath of sins' indwelling, the scars, consequences, and memories are not wiped out in an altar crisis, they are carried over into the cleansed and Christ-indwelt life. These will be refined and rectified by growing in grace and maturing in holiness.

"When the work is done, 'tis but begun."

The motivation is *"the fear of God."* This fear is not to be confused with fearfulness or terror. It is far from cowering servitude or shivering dread. It is the spelling, not of bondage but of freedom; not of gloom but of gladness; for we are to serve the Lord with fear and rejoice!

This fear is a sense of awe and reverence. There is always the concern that we do nothing displeasing to God, but, as stated above, it has a much deeper meaning. Having been made partakers of His nature, we naturally adopt His attitude toward sin. What affects God now affects us, and what stirs Him to the depth is not suffering, but sin. The Spirit-filled Christian will have a burning devotion for God and holiness and a flaming aversion for sin and unholiness. It has been said that the essence of fear is "perception," and perception further implies "sensitiveness," and that is the essential content of fear. It is thus that we discover that fear is the beginning of wisdom as it carries with it the desire and sensitivity to follow the lead of our Lord and *"always do those things that please Him"* (John 8:29).

7

Spiritual Liberty
(Romans 8:1-11)

Much has been taught concerning the vicarious suffering of Christ who bore our sins on the cross and as is recorded in Isaiah 63:3, "I have trodden the winepress alone." He was God's propitiation for the sins of the world. He's the Lamb of God that takes away the sin of the world. However, while we are quite willing to accept Him as our substitute, we are very reticent to experientially identify ourselves with Him and His cross.

The hymn writer said it correctly when he wrote the lyrics to his song:

"Must Jesus bear the cross alone, and all the world go free?
No, there's a cross for everyone, and there's a cross for me."

We often speak of trouble, trials, sicknesses, and such as being a cross to bear, and they are burdensome, but Jesus informs us that only His follower can bear the cross, and one must bear it voluntarily. Therefore, the cross we bear cannot mean any of the trials and tribulations we face because even those who are not His followers endure those things.

While His cross speaks of substitution, it also requires our identification. While there was a cross erected on Calvary, there must also be one erected in the heart of the Christian if salvation is to be effective. The same Christ that declared, *"Except a man be born again, he cannot see the kingdom of God,"* (John 3:3). also declared with equal authority and truth, *"Except a corn of wheat fall in the ground and die, it abideth alone: but if it die, it bringeth forth much fruit"* (John 3:3, 12:24 KJV). There is much taught about the new birth, but little or nothing is said concerning the subsequent crucifixion of the "**old man**," the carnal mind.

We speak directly or indirectly about imputed righteousness of Christ but seldom about the imparted righteousness of Christ. We would rather talk about being "holy-in-Christ" while vile and sinful in ourselves. This has become a major dividing line in theological thought. Adam Clarke, the brilliant Methodist Theologian, states with sound, scriptural logic, "Righteousness imputed, righteousness imparted, and righteousness practiced, are always found together. God never imputes unless He imparts and imparted righteousness immediately withers when not practiced."

The very first verse of this passage, by implication, speaks volumes concerning the freedom that comes from being crucified with Christ. *"There is therefore **NOW** no condemnation to those who are in Christ Jesus, who do not walk according to the flesh, but according to the Spirit"* (Romans 8:1). The word "**NOW**" brings us up to a present state of spirituality where there is no displeasure of God resting on the soul; there is no conscience reality of a condition that is at enmity (hostile) against God. There is nothing out of harmony with God.

Therefore, this being true, there must be such a state of grace in this present world where one is "truly" free from all sin. The only source from whence condemnation comes to the soul is through one's own personal sin problem. One is not condemned because he is sick, infirm, feeble, ignorant, or because he suffers any lack or limitations in his humanity. "Our infirmities may be grounds for our humiliation but not condemnation; only sin can bring condemnation upon the soul."[16]

It therefore follows that if there is a possibility and place in this present world where there is no condemnation resting on the soul, it is only because that soul has found a complete solution to the sin problem (both disobedience and depravity) in the divine plan of salvation.

---

16   Dr. Harry Jessop, *Foundations of Doctrine*, Pg 116

The Law of the Spirit of Life vs The Law of Sin and Death

The Bible is full of paradoxes. The dictionary defines "paradox" as "a statement that appears to contradict itself or be contrary to common sense but that may be true." The Scriptures teach us that according as we suffer we shall reign; we must humble ourselves if we ever expect to be exalted. In order to be free from the old law we must yield unreservedly to the new law; we must choose to be enslaved in order to be emancipated, and we must die in order to live.

Following the grain-of-wheat principle that Jesus gave in John 12:25, He says, *"He who loves his life will lose it, and he who hates his life in this world will keep it for eternal life."* I recall hearing Dr. Eldon Fhurman say in a sermon, in reference to this verse, "You must die; if you don't die you will die, but if you will die you won't die." There is a death to flee and a death to pursue. The death we must pursue is the death to the sinful ego, the "BIG I," that demands its rights to itself against God. "This 'BIG I' is seen to be nothing other than the 'law of sin,' the 'carnal mind,' and the 'evil heart of unbelief,' with the mask off."[17] As Paul gave his own personal testimony in Galatians 2:20, *"I have been crucified with Christ; it is no longer I who live, but Christ lives in me."*

Here we have two conflicting laws, the law of the Spirit of life and the law of sin and death. Life emanates from one, and death is the end result of the other. From the former, life flows from the Spirit and from the latter, death issues from sin.

In this Epistle, the word "law" is used in various ways. Sometimes it is spoken of as a statute or commandment. It acts as a schoolmaster to bring men and women to Christ. The law, in this context, is a standard of living, but in itself, it has no capacity to enable one to abide by its standard. It shouts its commands, "thou shalt" and "thou shalt not," but it offers no power to obey them.

---

17 Richard S. Taylor, *Life in the Spirit*, Pg. 52

Paul says, *"I was alive once without the law, but when the commandment came, sin revived and I died"* (Romans 7:9). The commandment has the power to convict but not convert. It is like a mirror that can reveal the dirt on your face, but lacks the power to remove it, or like a plumb line that can disclose that a wall is out of square, but cannot bring it into alignment. That is one use of the word "law."

When he speaks of the **law of the Spirit** or the **law of sin and death**, he uses the word law as a mighty force or trend, as a ruling principle. It is a ruling principle such as the law of centrifugal force or the law of gravitation. For example, when an item is dropped, it naturally falls to the ground because the law of gravitation always trends that way. As the writer declares, *"For I delight in the law of God according to the inward man, but I see another law in my members, warring against the law of my mind, and bringing me into captivity to the law of sin which is in my members"* (Romans 7:22-23). Just as the law of gravitation renders any dropped object helpless from falling to the ground, the law of sin renders one powerless to free himself from sin.

Astronauts have discovered a higher law, the law of levitation. The law of levitation has made me free from the law of gravitation. There is gravity out there. If the space craft doesn't keep flying, it will start falling. But as long as it keeps moving, there is no feeling of gravity at all. The higher law has overcome the lower law. Paul is saying that the law of sin brought death, but the law of the Spirit brings life in Christ. But we have to keep walking in the light. [18]

"For what the law could not do in that it was weak through the flesh, God did by sending His own Son in the likeness of sinful flesh, on account of sin: He condemned sin in the flesh" (Romans 8:3). Jesus is a God-sent man because there was heaven's authority behind Him. We see the great price for our redemption when we read, *"He who did not spare His own Son, but delivered Him up for us all"* (Romans 8:32). He shared Him with us all as a sin-offering in order to

---

18   Dr. Dale M. Yocum, *Fruit unto Holiness,* Pgs. 96-100

condemn sin in humanity. When He died on the cross, He passed a death sentence upon the sin in the soul.

God considers sin a criminal who committed high treason against the Government of God. The carnal mind is irreconcilable and will not submit or be subordinate to the law of God, neither indeed can be. It is entirely, absolutely, and eternally a criminal, and God will not compromise with it. He condemned it to death, and it must face crucifixion. It is our responsibility to surrender the "**old man**," the "**carnal mind**," the "**sin that dwells in me**," or whatever name you subscribe to it for execution. We are not responsible for this inbred, inborn sin within, but if we refuse to confess and renounce its presence, if we reject its cleansing, or if we excuse or in any way condone its existence in our soul, we will then be held accountable and suffer condemnation for it, and if we persist, we will perish with it.

He must extirpate the sin if He ever emancipates the soul. He pardons the sinner in response to his repentance (a sorrowful confession and total renunciation) and faith, but he cannot pardon (forgive) the carnal mind because it is ever and always enmity against God and must be purged, cleansed, crucified or destroyed. The Holy Spirit meets and masters our lives in the depths. This inner, deeper experience, through the law of the Spirit of Life in Christ Jesus liberates us from the former power that had enslaved us, the law of sin and death.

We now are not only free from the sin of disobedience in our practical life and indwelling sin within, but we are free from the disposition to sin. Those in the Spirit are no longer disposed to sin as we read, *"For those who live according to the flesh **set their minds on** (are disposed to) the things of the flesh, but those who live according to the Spirit, (are disposed to) the things of the Spirit"* (Romans 8:5).

There are those who question God's ability and man's capacity to be free from all sin. Everlasting life is contingent on being saved from all sin. Let me share an illustration from a holiness preacher of another day.

If one would approach me and say, "I have found the fountain of youth. I have found the secret of how one can live 'physically' forever." I would suggest to him that if I am going to believe his proposition, it would first be necessary for him to explain to me how he resolved the problem concerning whatever it was that previously caused me to die. If he could not explain to me how he resolved that problem then I would have no faith his proposition.

So it is with those who preach the Gospel and yet deny that God can save from all sin in this present world. Because man, as the result of sin, is under the sentence of death, *"for the wages of sin is death"* (Romans 6:23), if their god does not deliver them from all sin in this life, I am not interested in their message. The Bible teaches us, *"He is also able to save to the uttermost those who come to God through Him, since He always lives to make intercession for them"* (Hebrews 7:25). This chapter begins with no condemnation and ends with no separation, and throughout it teaches us that if condemnation is lifted from us by the law of the Spirit, then our days here on earth should be lived out through life in the Spirit. *"The law of the Spirit of life in Christ Jesus hath made me free from the law of sin and death,"* not only in the well remembered crises of the new birth and in entire sanctification, but also by His indwelling Presence in the daily conflicts involved in holy and righteous living.

8

Pentecost: The Consequence of Calvary
(Acts 2:1-4)

The Day of Pentecost is the greatest day between Christ's resurrection and His return. From the time that man, through disobedience fell in the Garden, the whole plan of God was to return him to His creator, and man was to be the habitat of God, the place of His dwelling. God's plan was to eventually come back into man's heart and make him the Temple of the living God.

Immediately after the fall of man in the Garden, God initiated His plan of redemption and restoration. *"So the Lord God said to the serpent: Because you have done this, you are cursed more than all cattle, And more than every beast of the field; on your belly you shall go, and you shall eat dust all the days of your life. And I will put enmity between you and the woman, and between your seed and her seed; He shall bruise your head. And you shall bruise His heel"* (Genesis 3:14-15).

In the Old Testament, God's early method of leading His people was by directly appearing to the patriarchs, and through them, God would communicate His message. For example, God appeared to Abram at various times concerning various events that would occur in his life. God made a covenant with Abram, and the sign of that covenant was that every male child should be circumcised. Again, *"When Abram was ninety-nine years old, the Lord appeared to Abram and said to him, 'I am Almighty God; walk before me and be blameless"* (Genesis 17:1). God later gave Abraham the promise, that in spite of his age, he and Sarah would have a son, and He even told them to call his name Isaac. (Genesis 17:15-19). Later God commanded Abraham to offer his son Isaac as a burnt offering in the land of Moriah. There on the mountain, as painful as it must have been, Abraham obeyed God's command unreservedly, and God gave Isaac back to him. God, in Isaac's stead, provided a ram that was caught in the thicket as an offering. Because of Abraham's total devotion, God said, *"Blessing I will bless you, and multiplying I will multiply your descendants as the stars of the heaven and as the sand is on the seashore; and your descendants shall possess the gate of their enemies. In your seed all the nations of the earth shall be blessed, because you have obeyed my voice"* (Genesis 22:17-18).

In Exodus, Chapter 3, God spoke to Moses from the midst of a bush that was on fire, but not consumed, and gave him instructions to deliver His people out of the land of Egypt where they had been slaves to the taskmaster Pharaoh. God was with Moses when he confronted Pharaoh with the various plagues, and the God of the Hebrews defeated the gods of the Egyptians each time until Pharaoh let the children of Israel go. God led Moses, with the rod, across the Red Sea where they were safe from Pharaoh's armies.

The people were to go over and possess the land of Canaan, but instead of following God's directives, they sent out twelve men to spy out the land. They brought back an evil report, except for Joshua and Caleb, and refused to go up and possess the land as God had told them. Because of their disobedience they wandered forty years in the wilderness. Moses was constantly confronted with problems such as the scarcity of water and no food, but worst of all, he had to deal with a murmuring and complaining people.

God met Moses on Mount Sinai and gave him the tables of stone, called the Ten Commandments. When he came off the mountain, he had to confront a rebellious people again who had molded a golden calf from their jewelry, an idol in which to worship. On each occasion God directed Moses, and he, in turn, directed the people.

Time and again God spoke to the people through the patriarchs of the faith. God's Presence followed them in a cloud by day and pillar of fire by night. He later instructed the building of the Tabernacle, and God's Presence dwelt in the holy of holies, and He spoke through the priesthood. He also spoke to the fathers by the prophets.

Throughout this process, God was moving closer and closer to man whom He dearly loved, but He was not as close as He planned to be.

The writer of the Hebrew letter tells us, *"He spoke in times past to the fathers by the prophets, has in these last days spoken to us by His Son"* (Hebrews 1:1). God has been speaking at various times in various ways even through the majesty of creation itself. The Scriptures tell us, *"The heavens declare the glory of God; and the firmament shows His handiwork. Day unto day utters speech, and night unto night reveals knowledge. There is no speech nor language where their voice is not heard"* (Psalms 19:1-3). The very heaven of the heavens is a revelation of God.

C. S. Lewis said, "You can know more about someone by listening to his words than you can by looking at the house he built." While the creation tells us a lot about the Creator, and while we learned a great deal about Him through the Prophets, God wanted to say something to us that neither creation, nor a poet, nor a prophet could say. Therefore, God spoke that word in His Son when the *"Word became flesh and dwelt among us, and we beheld His glory, the glory of the only begotten of the Father, full of grace and truth"* (John 1:14).

John tells us in his Gospel, *"No one has seen God at any time. The only begotten Son, who is in the bosom of the Father, He has declared Him"* (John 1:18). The word "declared" means exegeted, implying that Jesus made it possible that God the Father might be known to all. If one is ever asked what God is like, all he has to do is point them to Jesus. Philip said to Jesus, *"Lord, show us the Father, and it is sufficient for us." Jesus said to him, "Have I been with you so long, and yet you have not known me, Philip? He who has seen Me has seen the Father; so how can you say, 'Show us the Father'?"*

The incarnate Christ came into this world not only to reveal to us the Father, *"He was manifested to take away our sins and in Him there is no sin,"* John also says, *"For this purpose the Son of God was manifested, that He might destroy the works of the devil"* (I John 3:5, 8). The purpose of His coming was to free man from all sin by the sacrifice of Himself. As the Lamb of God, He provided a sinless sac-

57

rifice for the sin of the world. The efficacy of the cross is now available to save man from disobedience, defilement, and depravity. *"He Himself is the propitiation for our sins, and not for ours only but also for the whole world"* (1 John 2:2). He came to reveal the Father, redeem us from all sin, and restore man to his lost estate by, *"putting on the new man which was created according to God in true righteousness and holiness"* (Ephesians 4:24).

Following His resurrection He ascended back to the right hand of the Father. He had promised His disciples before He left them that He would not leave them orphans, but He would send the Holy Spirit unto them. *"I will pray the Father, and He will give you another Helper,* (Comforter-Paraclete) *that He may abide with you forever—the Spirit of truth, whom the world cannot receive, because it neither sees Him nor knows Him; but you know Him, for He dwells with you and will be in you. I will not leave you orphans; I will come to you"* (John 14:16-18). He had earlier given the same promise to all that would come to Him. *"If anyone thirst, let him come to me and drink. He who believes in me, as the Scripture has said, out of his heart will flow rivers of water."* (Following this invitation, in the next verse He gives us the interpretation.) *"By this He spoke concerning the Spirit, whom those believing in Him would receive; for the Holy Spirit was not yet given, because Jesus was not yet glorified"* (John 7:37-39).

Following His resurrection Luke tells us, *"He presented Himself alive after His suffering by many infallible proofs, being seen by them during forty days and speaking of the things pertaining to the kingdom"* (Acts 1:3). Just previous to His ascension to heaven, back to the Father's right hand where He is glorified, He gives His last command to those believers who were assembled in the upper room in Jerusalem. *"Wait for the promise of the Father, which, He said, you have heard from me. For John truly baptized with water, but you shall be baptized with the Holy Spirit not many days from now"* (Acts 1:4-5).

On that inaugural Day of Pentecost, recorded in the second Chapter of Acts, the one hundred and twenty in the upper room received the promised blessing. Jesus, through the Holy Spirit, had come back to dwell in the hearts of man. He finally was able to take up residency in man's heart, and man again became the temple of His dwelling. The separation and alienation that came about through the fall in the Garden where man became estranged from his Creator had finally ended.

The long journey that God made to bring man back to Himself had now come to fruition. God began communicating with man in various ways, through the patriarchs of old, the tabernacle and the priesthood, by the clouds that led them by day and the fire that led them by night, speaking from the mountain, through the prophets, up until the Word became flesh and dwelt among us here on earth. All of this was preparatory for the time when He would enter into His rightful abode in the heart of every man who will welcome Him. This is why Jesus said to His disciples, *"Nevertheless I tell you the truth. It is to your advantage that I go away; for if I do not go away, the Helper will not come to you; but if I depart, I will send Him to you"* (John 16:7).

Consider some of the principles which support the great pillars of our Christian faith. If Christ had not been born, there would not have been an acceptable sacrifice for man's sin upon Calvary's cross. If Christ had not risen from the dead, the cross would have been the world's greatest tragedy and our faith would be in vain, and we would still be in our sin. Without Christ's ascension, there would have been no Pentecost. Without Pentecost, there would never have been a fulfillment of the grand redemptive scheme.

> The end of Christ's incarnation, life, death, and resurrection was to prepare a holy nature for us in Himself, which nature is imparted to us by His indwelling us. Our holiness is never an attainment in our own power, but always a gift. It inheres in Him, not in us, and we possess it only while we retain Him.[19]

Pentecost validated and authenticated that redemption for the world was complete and available to all who will receive Him.

---

19 Joe Brice, Pentecost, Pg. 32, Quoting Marshall's book: *The Gospel Mystery of Sanctification*

While we of this 21st century were not there in the flesh when Jesus was crucified and we were not the ones to whom He appeared alive after His passion, we are able to validate the resurrection of Christ by our own personal Pentecost when Christ is enthroned within our hearts by His Spirit.

Purity of Pentecost

Jesus knew that if His disciples were going to carry on the work that He had begun while on earth, they needed the baptism with the Holy Spirit. The entire Godhead is equally involved in man's redemption. God, the Father, conceived the plan of salvation to save man from all sin. Sin is not only an act but also a disease; the act needs forgiven and the disease needs cleansed. Jesus, through His death and resurrection, filled the prescription for the malady of the soul, and now the Holy Spirit, as the executive of the Godhead is here to administer the remedy.

The church before Pentecost had within it a principle which antagonized their Christian graces and issued in fear, selfish ambition, resentment, and spiritual impotence. Certain affections of the world-life from which Christ had called them still subsisted with primitive Christian graces within their hearts. There was a conflict within. Jesus had to rebuke their unbelief, correct their gross conceptions of His kingdom, reprove their selfish ambitions, and restrain their personal resentments. They lived in a powerfully pagan world, the world that had made Calvary, and they were patently powerless to affect it for good. We see them at last gathered behind closed doors, a wistful company of disciples, paralyzed by fear and the menace of disillusion. But their presence there is the sure witness that they were conscience of their need of something better. Then came Pentecost."[20]

The Holy Spirit came like a refining fire and cleansed the heart of the carnal mind. Just as when the light is turned on, the darkness

---

20 Joe Brice, *Pentecost* Pgs. 20-21

flees; when the Holy Spirit comes in, sin moves out. Purity of heart is the essential element of the Pentecostal experience.

By purity of heart we mean that which is undefiled, untainted, free from evil stains, without earthly alloy. It is holiness unmixed with selfishness and pride, or any other polluting or debasing element. When this supernatural and divine work is wrought in us by the Holy Spirit, all the chaff, refuse, and dross are purged away and sifted out of the soul, and the precious residue is the genuine, the true, the pure and the good.[21]

It is the pure heart that enables the Christian to "BE" the witness that the world desperately needs. *"Keep your heart with all diligence, for out of it springs the issues of life"* (Proverbs 4:23). One's conduct is always a reflection of his character. The question is asked, *"Does a spring send forth fresh water and bitter from the same opening"* (James 3:11). The experience of Pentecost was the cleansing of the heart from all sin so that the world could behold the beauty of holiness. *"Now the purpose of the commandment is love from a pure heart"* (I Timothy 1:5).

Power of Pentecost

There used to be a Pure Oil Company whose motto was, "**Be sure with Pure**." The more oil is refined the more powerful it is. This is a good motto for one whose heart is pure. There is power in purity. The power is not apart from the Person of the Holy Spirit Himself; power is always inherent in Him, not in us. *"You shall receive power when the Holy Spirit is come upon you; and you shall be witnesses to Me in Jerusalem, and in all Judea and Samaria, and to the end of the earth"* (Acts 1:8).

The Holy Spirit is the *"Paraclete"*—one called alongside to help. On the Day of Pentecost, the disciples were endued, by the Holy Spirit's presence, with a power they had never experienced before. The achievements of that day were so extraordinary that it

---

21 Thomas Cook, *New Testament Holiness* Pg. 33

caused those who were looking on to ask, *"Whatever could this mean?"* (Acts 2:12). After Peter delivered his message, *"that day about three thousand souls were added to the church and the Lord added to the church daily those who were being saved"* (Acts 2:41, 47).

It not only gave them an emancipated personality through the cleansing of the heart from the defilement of sin, it also gave them an enlightened perspective that they had never known before. Jesus told them that when the Holy Spirit came, He would guide them into all truth. Peter was able to understand prophecies (Joel 2:28-32) that before were a mystery to him. We will never know more about God, the Father, or Jesus, His Son, than the Spirit teaches us. He comes to teach, instruct, enlighten, endue, and empower us.

"Oh, my heart, be still before Him.
Prostrate, inwardly adore Him!"

Not only were they able to perceive and understand that which before were mysteries to them, they were able to preach with great power and authority, and they were able to prevail in the midst of tremendous persecution. Previous to Pentecost, Peter denied his Lord; Thomas doubted Him; they all fled and forsook Him, but after Pentecost cowardice gave way to boldness; selfishness yielded to humility; love was made pure and perfect, and doubt was exchanged for assurance.

It is in the experience of the grace of Pentecost that the swaddling clothes of spiritual babyhood are exchanged for the stature of adulthood in spiritual things. That which involves a time element and disciplinary processes in the realm of our natural development is changed instantly in our spiritual life. We are made alive spiritually by the new birth, and we are brought to adulthood spiritually by the Spirit's baptism. There is a place for the element of time and discipline in the maturing of the Christian character but not in the facts of saving one from all sin.

The two works of grace which constitute full fledged Christianhood are essential as a preparation for normal growth and development in the Christian life. Let us therefore exalt the grace of Pentecost, recognizing that it is an essential part of our salvation.[22]

The Holy Spirit is permitted to fully possess our lives. He is the agent that fires our passion for souls, quickens our obedience, empowers our praying, unctionizes our preaching and singing, anoints our testimonies, and gives us the courage and willingness to serve and suffer, if need be, for Jesus.

When we are baptized with the Holy Spirit, our heart is cleansed of the carnal mind, the disposition that is *"enmity against God; for it is not subject to the law of God, nor indeed can be"*(Romans 8:7). Christ, through His Spirit, is enthroned in the heart. He rules and reigns without a rival. He is both Savior and Lord. When fully submitted to Him as Lord, whatever He desires of us will never be challenged by us.

> In the Christian Gospel the believer stands so related to Christ that Christ's commands never come to him as bare commands, standing alone; rather do they come to him as **implied** promises. Christ never asks the impossible. To be sure, He often asks the **humanly** impossible. There would be no meaning in His mission as the Divine Redeemer if He does for us no more than we could do for ourselves. Here indeed is the critical point where the glory of the Gospel blazes out; Christ asks for more than we can supply and then proceeds to furnish the difference Himself. It was Augustine who once prayed; "O God give what thou commandest, and then command what thou wilt."[23]

Pentecost is indeed the consequence of the death and resurrection of Christ. He now sits at the right hand of the Father making intercession for us as the great High Priest. His glorification made Pentecost possible. The Christian life begins at Calvary, but effective Christian service begins when we have a personal Pentecost and are filled with the Holy Spirit. Someone has well said that when

---

22 Dr. C. W. Butler, *The Christian Witness*, May 20, 1943
23 Dr. Paul S. Rees, *The American Holiness Journal*, September 1965

Jesus preached the Sermon on the Mount, it was Christianity made practical, but without Pentecost it would be paralyzing. Let us not stop at Calvary, but press on to Pentecost, thereby not allowing Christ's death for our sanctification be in vain.

9

The More Excellent Way
(I Corinthians 13)

The church of Corinth was the Apostle Paul's greatest problem church. Because of their spiritual babyhood, they were inundated with envy, strife, and divisions. He was the agent of the Holy Spirit acting as an administrator, trying delicately to dispense the truth and direct their activities. It required both admonition and gentle rebuke to accomplish his labor of love amongst them.

Sanctification carries two distinct ideas, that of separation and that of purification. The Apostle Paul is writing *"to the church of God which is at Corinth, to those who are sanctified in Christ Jesus, called to be saints"* (I Corinthians 1:2). In this verse, the idea of separation is the true meaning of sanctification. It is often referred to as "initial" sanctification. Also, because they have a saving relationship with Christ, they are designated as "saints." They are the "called out ones," who have separated themselves from the world, and they have a spiritual relationship to Jesus Christ. They were justified by faith and have peace with God. But while there is now no condemnation resting upon them, the remains of carnality are prevalent within them.

They were babes in Christ and needed to *"go on unto perfection"* (Hebrews 6:1).

In the second and third chapters of this letter, Paul identifies humanity in one of three stages of life:

1. The *natural* man (2:14)
2. The *carnal* man (2:15)
3. The *spiritual* man (3:1)

The natural man is the man who has no relationship with Christ. He is the man who is lost and without hope in this world. The Apostle says, *"The things of the Spirit of God are foolishness to him."* This man has no spiritual discernment and no ability to properly judge truth from error, and because of his unbelief, he is totally void of the *"mind of the Lord that he may instruct him"* (I Corinthians 2:14-16).

The carnal man had been born again and was a babe in Christ. He lives his life on the level of faith, but it was mixed with selfishness. Spiritually, his diet was only food that a baby could digest because he is in a state of protracted infancy. He lacked the spiritual discernment to be able to grasp the deep truths that the spiritual man could understand. He manifests a dual-mindedness. His life is characterized by a little girl's prayer: "Lord, make the bad people good; and please Lord, make the good people nice." Carnal Christians are good, in the sense that they have faith in Christ and the root of discipleship in them, but so often, as in the community of believers in Corinth, they do not act the "nice" part of Christ-mindedness.[24]

The spiritual man represents life that is lived on the level of love, under the mastery of the Holy Spirit. He could not be satisfied with a constant "milk diet" because in his heart he was hungry for the "solid meat" of full surrender, of Christian holiness. He has experienced not only the birth of the Spirit, but also the baptism with the Spirit. He has entered into the **"more excellent"** way.

It was because the Corinthian Christians lingered too long in spiritual infancy that problems began to erupt. We will list a few of the major problems that were the result of the failure of these "babes in Christ" to go on unto the level of pure love. Allow me to once again quote C. W. Butler from the previous chapter concerning babes in Christ:

> It is in the experience of the grace of Pentecost that the swaddling clothes of spiritual babyhood are exchanged for the

---

24   Paul S. Rees, Sermon: "St Paul's Three Men"

stature of adulthood in spiritual things. That which involves a time element and disciplinary processes in the realm of our natural development is changed instantly in our spiritual life. (The full statement can be read in the previous chapter.)

They had what some would call "preacher's religion," as each one was following their favorite spiritual leader. The Apostle Paul said that each of them had their unique work and ministries, but God is the one who gives the increase. *"For we are God's fellow workers; you are God's field, you are God's building. According to the grace of God which was given to me, as a wise master builder I have laid the foundation, and another builds on it. For no other foundation can anyone lay than that which is laid, which is Jesus Christ"* (I Corinthians 3:9-11).

These Christians were coming out of a culture that religiously engaged in sensuality and debauchery. Venus, the goddess of love, i.e., lust, was worshipped there more extravagantly than anywhere else in the world. There was incestuous fornication that was a grave contamination to the church. *"It is actually reported that there is sexual immorality among you, and such sexual immorality as is not even named among the Gentiles—that a man has his father's wife"* (I Corinthians 5:1). Paul had to teach the principles of marriage and its sacredness. He taught the role and responsibility of a husband to his wife and wife to her husband, and the Christian principles that apply to the unmarried and the widows.

He was warning them of the idolatry of offering meat to idols or eating the meat that was previously offered to idols. He rebuked those who spoke as though they were so knowledgeable. While knowledge is a gift of the Spirit and is very valuable, without being governed by divine love (*agape*), it is dangerous, as it will induce spiritual pride which normally comes before a fall. Great light without great love is always dangerous.

He tells them that the real danger is not *"eating things offered to idols,* (because) *we know that an idol is nothing in the world, and that there is no other God but one"* (I Corinthians 8:4). It is here that he teaches that no man lives to himself nor dies to himself, but that we have a stewardship of influence to protect. It will not adversely affect the one eating that which was offered to the idol, but in so doing it may *"become a stumbling block to those who are weak"*... *"Therefore, if food makes my brother stumble, I will never again eat meat, lest I make my brother stumble"* (I Corinthians 8:9, 13). Here the Apostle lays down a Christian principle which simply teaches that my own personal spiritual liberty must not take precedence over the well-being of a weaker brother.

He teaches them how to properly conduct themselves at the Lord's supper. He was teaching the real meaning of the occasion because some had become gluttonous and drunkards at this most sacred event. In instituting this sacred rite, he said it was a time of self-examination to see if they were worthy to partake. The purpose of eating the broken bread and drinking of the cup was to remember the sacrifice that He made for man's salvation until He comes again. Oswald Chambers said, "God is looking for men and women to become broken bread and poured out wine through whom God can work to meet the desperate need of a desperately needy world." It is thus that we are to identify with this great Christian rite.

When he comes to the twelfth chapter, he teaches concerning the diversity of the Gifts of the Spirit. He not only taught concerning their proper use, but he warned them concerning their abuse. Some were abusing the gifts of the Spirit, and Paul was there to correct their method of use. The Christian life has two dimensions to it; the inner and the outer dimension. To state it another way, the inner part of life concerns his character, and the outer part concerns the conduct. The baptism with the Holy Spirit solves both realms.

Purity of the heart is essential for man's devout "BEING" or his character. The indwelling Power of the Person of the Holy Spirit is essential for man's devoted "DOING" of his conduct. We have a tendency to emphasize one to the exclusion of the other. If we emphasize the inner "being" and exclude the outer "doing" it will lead to antinomianism, or lawlessness. On the other hand, if we emphasize the outer "doing" and exclude the inner "being" it will lead to an empty legalism or Pharisaism.

The two are inseparable. There can be no holy ethics in the life without the experience of holiness in the heart, but neither can the root long survive unless it bears fruit. Therefore, both the gifts of the Spirit and the fruit of the Spirit are essential to an effective and fruitful Christian life.

The gifts are *"distributed to each one individually* (severally) *as He wills"* (I Corinthians 12:11). A gift received is not a credit to the recipient as though he/she earned it, but all the glory is given to God who gave it. We are not responsible for its possession, only for its development. Along with the gifts of the Spirit comes the grace of love with all of its expressions and its fruit. True holiness not only frees from all sin; it is an unfolding of the fruit of the Spirit.

The grace of **love** is the substratum and expression of the revealing fruits:

1. Joy is **love** blessing.
2. Peace is **love** blending.
3. Long-suffering is **love** bending.
4. Gentleness is **love** bestowing.
5. Goodness is **love** behaving.
6. Faithfulness is **love** believing.
7. Meekness is **love** bowing.
8. Temperance is **love** balancing.

Chapter 13 has been called the meat in the sandwich that was placed in between Chapters 12 and 14. Having finished his instructions concerning spiritual gifts, he admonishes them to *"earnestly desire the best gifts. And yet I show you a more excellent way"* (I Corinthians 12:31). The Corinthian believers had become puffed up over certain spiritual gifts. Paul was telling them not to major on the minor because in doing so, one will minor on the major. He pointed out, as important as the gifts of the Spirit were, they are secondary to something vastly more important, that being the grace of love.

Perhaps because we use the word "love" in such a broad sense, we need to define what Paul is speaking of in this chapter. He distinguishes the difference between human and divine love; **Agape**, meaning divine love and involving the whole matter of man's salvation, and **phila**, meaning human love, which has no salvation in it. Everybody has the latter, but the former love must be *"poured out in our hearts by the Holy Spirit who was given to us"* (Romans 5:5). It is the self-sacrificial nature of God, that love that Jesus demonstrated on the cross of Calvary when He saved others but not Himself.

In the first three verses of Chapter 13, the Apostle shows us love's **pre-eminence** when he lifts all the gifts to the zenith of their glory, and then says that minus this love, they are nothing. There must be the possibility of a loveless language speaking, loveless prophetic speaking, loveless knowledge, loveless faith, and loveless charity. We must not engage in these spiritual activities minus the love of God, for without love, it will have no eternal value and profit nothing. He desires our love more than our labor.

In the next four verses he speaks of the **proprieties** of this love. The practice and ethics of this love always enriches life.

Love alone can transform a house into a home, and lock the machinery of the divorce mills; it's the only thing that will settle the disputes and solve the difficulties between labor and management; it's the only thing that will purify the cesspools of politics, and make righteous leadership out of self-seeking politicians. It is the only thing that will give the heart of brotherhood to all ecclesiastical organizations, which purport to exalt the deity of our Savior and Redeemer, Jesus Christ, making of them colleagues instead of competitors.[25]

"Love suffers long and is kind; love does not envy; love does not parade itself, is not puffed up; does not behave rudely, does not seek its own, is not provoked, thinks no evil; does not rejoice in iniquity, but rejoices in truth; bears all things, believes all things, hopes all things, endures all things" (I Corinthians 13:4-7).

The one enduring element of Christianity is love, and he says *"It will never fail." "Whether there are prophecies, they will fail; whether there are tongues, they will cease; whether there is knowledge, it will vanish away. For we know in part and we prophecy in*

---

25 S. H. Turbeville, Sermon preached at Sychar Camp, Ohio, 1951)

part. But when that which is perfect has come, then that which is in part will be done away....And now abide faith, hope, love, these three; but the greatest of these is love. " (I Corinthians 13:8-10, 13)

Faith is the foundation of Christianity; hope is the anticipation, but love is the realization of the Christ-like life. The more excellent way is love, for love believes hopes and abides. While this love is perfect in quality, it must ever increase in quantity. Paul writing to the Thessalonians prayed that, *"the Lord would make them increase and abound in love to one another and to all, just as we do to you, so that He may establish your hearts blameless in holiness before our God and Father at the coming of our Lord Jesus Christ with all His saints"* (I Thessalonians 3:12-13).

If we do not faithfully and obediently walk in the light and continue to increase in our love capacity, there is a danger of leaking love out of our heart. Once while reading and studying, I came across an article that has been very enlightening and helpful to my own walk with God, and I want to share excerpts from that article with those who read these words.

Love is like a flame or volatile fluid; it is not like a rigid, fixed substance. It is ever in a fine, subtle motion, and needs constant feeding. A piece of wood is solid and stationary in its form, remaining the same year after year; but the soft quivering flame is very different. One may have a clear specific doctrine of sanctification (perfect love) fixed as an unchanging truth in your mind, and yet the quivering flame of love in your heart is another thing. Our emotions glide away imperceptibly; our affections leak out of the soul unawares.....
It requires much diligence and the adding of heart fuel to keep a lowly, loving flame in the soul. ... Those things which are the sweetest are susceptible of being turned into the most sour; and perfect love losing itself in the fermentation of spirit and turning sour is one of the harshest, bitter things on earth. ... It will take an immense amount of love to keep the gentleness and charity of the heart up equal to the sharp discernment of the mind. Mr. Wesley often observed that great light upon reli-

gious matters, without great love, was dangerous. We must keep the affections pure, and warm, and tender, at any cost."[26]

There are many things that we do not find ourselves qualified to say or do. We may not have the talent to sing, teach, preach, or many other things, but all have the God-given capacity to love. There is no loving wife who would accept any gifts or courtesies as a substitute for their husband's love and devotion. This love cannot give more and must not give less than the gift of itself. Jesus demonstrated this on the cross, and again I say that He is more jealous for your love than for your labor, money, talent or anything else. *"Earnestly desire the best gifts. And yet I show you a **MORE EXCELLENT WAY"** (I Corinthians 12:31).

---

26   G. D. Watson, Article in *Heart and Life*, February 1953

10

The Inheritance of the Saints
(Acts 26:12-18 and Ephesians 1:13-14)

In Acts Chapter 26, the Apostle Paul is recounting his conversion experience and his personal encounter with his Lord while on his journey to Damascus. In the other passage recorded in Ephesians 1:13-14, we have reference of the moment when the believer is sealed with the Holy Spirit of Promise. In both of these passages there is mention made of an **inheritance**.

In I Thessalonians 4:3, the same writer says, *"For this is the will of God, your sanctification."* The word **will** in the above scripture can be understood in at least three ways:

1. As a command from our Sovereign Ruler, it's the will of God.

2. The word "will," can speak of God's power or ability. What He wills, He can accomplish. *"Now to Him who is able to do exceedingly abundantly above all that we ask or think, according to the power that works in us"* (Ephesians 3:20).

3. But for the purpose of this chapter, I want to think of God as our Father and His "will" as our patrimony, our heritage, our legacy, our birthright.

In Acts Chapter 26, Paul is rehearsing the commission that God gave to him. He was to go to the Gentiles *"to open their eyes, in order to turn them from darkness to light, and from the power of Satan unto God, that they may receive forgiveness of sins and an inheritance among those who are sanctified by faith in me"* (Acts 26:18). Here we see that the inheritance that they were to receive was the fruit of sanctification, which is the will of God. It was to follow their conversion, and is conditioned on faith.

In Ephesians Chapter 1, we are told that it was after they had heard and believed the truth they were *"sealed with the Holy Spirit of Promise which was their guarantee (earnest) of inheritance until the redemption of the purchased possession, to the praise of His glory."* This seal is a symbol of ownership where God stamps His own divine (insignia) image on those who are His, and He never confuses them with the *"children of the devil"* (I John 3:10). The only ones who have the right to an inheritance are those who are members of the family. Therefore, when one is born of the Spirit, it is because he has heeded the call of God to *"come out from among them and be separate, says the Lord. Do not touch what is unclean, and I will receive you, and you shall be my sons and daughters, says the Lord Almighty"* (II Corinthians 6:17-18). He is adopted into God's family and becomes a rightful heir to an inheritance.

In response to the believer's consecration and faith, God sanctifies His children by the Baptism with the Holy Spirit of promise, "Thus marking him as God's purchased possession in Christ. This mark or seal is a bond between God and man as a sign of what we are and shall be to God, and of what He is and will be to us. It secures and assures. It stamps us as His possession and guarantees His kingdom and glory to us as our inheritance." [27]

The word *"guarantee,"* (translated *"earnest"* in KJV) is explained by Joseph Henry Thayer as "money which in purchases is given as a pledge that the full amount will subsequently be paid." It is a down payment we receive in this world that will be paid in full in the next world. It is a foretaste of the glory to come. It is a little of heaven down here while we are waiting for our final redemption over there.

However, an inheritance is useless unless it is claimed and possessed. Regardless of the generosity and liberality of the one who makes up the will, if one never claims his inheritance, it is as though there never was one to claim. I recall a story that was told of a widow and her son:

---

27 H. Orton Wiley and Ross E. Price, *The Epistle to the Ephesians*, Pg. 84

They had very little to live on and when the son became of age he enlisted in the armed forces. He told his mother that he would send money home each month for her to use to pay her bills. Several months later he got word that his mother was very ill and he needed to come home. Upon arriving home, he discovered that she was dying of pneumonia and malnutrition. When they found her, she had been living in a house with little or no heat, and there was nothing in her cupboards to eat. Her son was so heartbroken. He asked her what she had done with the allotment checks he had been sending home each month to provide for her care. She said, "Do you mean those green cards that I've been receiving through the mail that I used to seal up the cracks in the walls to keep the cold air out?" They discovered all the checks that he had been sending to her had been pasted on the walls because she never realized what a check was; she had always spent cash.

She was, in fact, financially very well off, but because she didn't realize what an allotment check was, she lived in abject poverty.

I'm convinced that many of God's children have been living like spiritual paupers because they have never claimed their rightful inheritance. There are many examples of this throughout God's Word, and I'd like to refer to one of them from the Old Testament.

God used Moses to lead the children of Israel out of their Egyptian bondage. Following the many battles and plagues that God brought upon Egypt, the day came when Moses led His children out. By the time Moses got to the Red Sea crossing, Pharaoh's armies were in pursuit to capture them and bring them back to Egypt. They were quite concerned because the enemy was pressing upon them, and the Red Sea was before them, and they were seemingly trapped. Moses petitioned God concerning their dilemma and God gave him instructions. *"Lift up your rod, and stretch out your hand over the sea and divide it. And the children of Israel shall go on dry ground through the midst of the sea"* (Genesis 14:16). Having crossed to safety on the other side of the sea, Pharaoh's armies tried to come across the sea, and God once again told Moses, *"Stretch out your hand over the sea, that the waters may come back upon the Egyptians, on their chariots, and on their horsemen. ... So the Lord overthrew the Egyptians in the midst of the sea"* (Genesis 14:26-27). They, once again, were the recipients of God's powerful deliverance.

Time and again God proved His faithfulness to the children of Israel. When He brought them out of Egypt, it was for the express purpose of bringing them into the Land of Canaan. There is a song with the lyrics, *"He bought me out, to bring me in, where shall I then His praise begin, freedom from sin, Canaan within, He brought me out to bring me in."* He did not bring them out of Egypt to have them wander aimlessly in the wilderness. They were to possess the Promised Land of Canaan, but through disobedience and unbelief, they wandered forty years in the wilderness, and all who came out of Egypt, except for Joshua and Caleb, were denied their inheritance.

Stephen tells us that, *"in their hearts they turned back to Egypt"* (Acts 7:39). Bodily they were in the wilderness, but in their hearts they longed for Egypt. It gives us pause for grave concern, as we consider how many have come to this crossroads. How many who have begun well, have now rejected the call to holiness, and while they are bodily in the church, their hearts are longing for the world.

"For the children of Israel walked forty years in the wilderness, till all the people who were men of war, who came out of Egypt, were consumed because they did not obey the voice of the Lord—to whom the Lord swore that He would not show them the land which the Lord had sworn to their fathers that He would give us, 'a land flowing with milk and honey.'" (Joshua 5:6).

While they were on the borders of Canaan, they refused to go in and possess it, but rather they sent out twelve men to spy out the land. When they returned, ten out of twelve of the spies brought back an evil report. These few men kept all the rest (except for Joshua and Caleb) from entering into the promised possession of Canaan. What a tragedy!

Just as holiness is the inheritance of the saints, Canaan was the inheritance of the Israelites. Holiness unclaimed is as unsatisfying as Canaan unpossessed. Canaan is a well-known type of holiness. When those ten spies brought back an evil report of the land, it prevented a multitude of people from entering therein. This illustrates for us how those who refuse to respond to God's call to holiness today can influence many others to reject God's call. We remind the reader that, *"He who rejects this (call to holiness) does not reject man, but God, who has also given us His Holy Spirit."* (I Thessalonians 4:8).

Let us look at the reasons they did not go into the land, keeping in mind that they all agreed on the goodness of the land. Let us also be aware, as previously stated, how a few critics and skeptics kept the Israelites from entering Canaan. Canaan being the inheritance of the Israelites is an Old Testament type of the New Testament truth concerning sanctification, which is the inheritance of the saints. Many are the skeptics and critics today, through their disobedience, that are hindering multitudes from receiving their birthright or inheritance that is due them.

They saw the land was full of giants. What giants loom large before many today that keep them from obeying the voice of God in His call to holiness? One of those giants is the *evil heart of unbelief.* The writer of the Hebrews is exhorting the believer to enter into the *"rest that remains for the people of God"* (Hebrews 4:9). In the previous chapter, he cautions us not to be like the children of Israel in the wilderness. He reminds us that it was through unbelief that they never entered the promised rest of Canaan. *"For whom, having heard, rebelled? Indeed, was it not all who came out of Egypt, led by Moses? Now with whom was He angry forty years? Was it not with those who sinned, whose corpses fell in the wilderness? And to whom did He swear that they would not enter His rest, but to those who did not obey? So we see that they could not enter in because of unbelief"* (Hebrews 3:16-19).

There are many who will give their evil reports and try to discourage others from entering into their promised rest of the soul and hinder them from heeding the call to holiness. A few such arguments are given below:

1. They received it all in conversion.

2. Man cannot be free from sin in this life; you sin every day in thought, word, or deed.
3. They will just have to grow and grow until they grow into holiness.
4. My former preacher didn't believe in it; why should I?
5. You will be free from sin when you die or after death in purgatory.

"Beware, brethren, lest there be in any of you an evil heart of unbelief in departing from the living God; but exhort one another daily, while it is called 'Today,' lest any of you be hardened through the deceitfulness of sin. (can be translated **'deceitfulness of sinners'**) *For we have become partakers of Christ if we hold the beginning of our confidence steadfast to the end, while it is said: 'Today, if you hear His voice, do not harden your hearts, as in the rebellion.* (Ps. 95:11; Hebrews 3:12-15).

We must have the courage to let God turn the searchlight on our soul and reveal the depths of our need. We then must be willing to face any barrier, deny any skeptic, and reject all the giants that come before us, whether by men or devils, and let God put them to flight, and we must claim our rightful heritage. Let us also remember that it was the minority, not the majority, of the twelve spies who were confident and put their faith in God's Word against all other voices and claimed the Promised Land. Joshua and Caleb initially said, *"Let us go up at once and possess the land."* Although they were denied access to the land for forty years, they were the only two who left Egypt who were permitted to enter in. Canaan finally became the land of the Israelites, not only by promise, but by possession. So, holiness promised becomes holiness possessed by believers who are willing to identify themselves as heirs of God's will and claim the *"guarantee"* of their inheritance.

11

Sanctify Them
(John 17:17)

When one comes down to the closing moments of his life, he doesn't engage in frivolous or trivial matters. He concerns himself with the most urgent and pressing issues. While Jesus never indulged in trivialities, it is certain that He now is concerned about things that were not only most important, but imperative. With His earthly life about to come to a conclusion, having finished the work which the Father had given Him to do, He is praying for those who were going to be continuing the work that He had begun while on earth. So this prayer has great significance for the early church, as well as the Christians today and the whole work of world evangelism.

He, who was the cornerstone of our salvation, would soon become the capstone when on the cross He looks to the Father and says, *"It is finished."* Following His resurrection, it will be a completion of the work that He had come to accomplish, but only the beginning of the work that He commissions all Spirit-filled believers to perform. In the first five verses of this chapter, He prayed for Himself concerning the suffering and death that was yet looming before Him. In the next fourteen verses, He prays for His disciples of that day, and the rest of the prayer is extended to all Christians of all time, including you and me.

We often seek the prayers of others who will intercede on our behalf to the Father. Jesus is the great Intercessor from whom we gladly and thankfully welcome His prayers. When Jesus prayed it was with absolute assurance that the Father would hear and answer. *"Father, I thank You that You have heard me. And I know that You always hear me"* (John 11:41-42). Here is God, the Son, praying to God, the Father, on behalf of His saints.

This prayer has been called the "High Priestly" prayer and since He has ascended to the Father's right hand, He is continuing His ministry as our advocate, pleading our cause to the Father. It is comforting to know that He is concerned for my welfare, as though there was no one else with whom to concern Himself. Jesus represents our cause to the Father and He represents the Father's concern to us. He tells us that the will of God is our sanctification, and in response to our need, He prays the Father to *"sanctify them by your truth; your word is truth"* (John 17:17). Let us look at the Who, What and Why of the recipients of the Lord's Prayer.

WHO: Their Identity

In this entire prayer, Jesus makes it very clear that He is praying for the believer (regenerate) and not for the world (unregenerate). Evidence is given throughout this prayer concerning that fact. I will list a few things that reveal that fact:

1. They had been given to Jesus by the Father (vs. 6, 9, 11).
2. They had obtained eternal life (vs. 2).
3. He had manifested the divine unto them because they were spiritual; the world receives no such manifestation (vs. 6).
4. They belonged to God in a very peculiar sense (vs. 6, 9).
5. They had been obedient to God, *"they have kept your word"* (vs. 6).
6. Christ had entrusted His truth with them as He was about to leave this world (vs. 8, 14).
7. Jesus was glorified in them (vs. 10).
8. Jesus had kept them from apostasy (vs. 12).
9. They were not of the world, but they were as separate from it as Jesus Himself (vs. 14, 16).
10. The world hated them because they were of another world (vs. 14)
11. They had already received, in a portion, of His glory (vs. 22).

If these for whom Jesus prayed were not true believers, then we are hard pressed to know what qualities characterize a true believer. In Verse 3 Jesus gives to us the definition of eternal life and says, *"That they may know you, the only true God, and Jesus Christ whom You have sent."* This makes "eternal life" an intimate knowledge of Him whose life is communicated to them.

Jesus says, *"I pray for them. I do not pray for the world but for those whom You have given Me, for they are Yours"* (John 17:9). He further prays, *"I do not pray that You should take them out of the world, but that You should keep them from the evil one"* (John 17:15). They were taken out of the world system. While they were no longer a part of the world's system and spirit, their presence was needed in the world to serve and even suffer, if need be, for the world's salvation. Their office work was to be God's ambassadors to the world. It is this world that God so loved that *"He gave His only begotten Son, that whosoever believes in Him should not perish but have everlasting life."* (John 3:16).

Even though there is voluminous evidence that they had been born again, there was also evidence that they still had the sinful nature. This sinful nature is revealed in various incidents recorded in the Gospels:

1. Such as, *"now there was also a dispute among them, as to which of them should be considered the greatest"* (Luke 22:24).
2. When Jesus was arrested in Gethsemane it is said that, *"They all forsook Him and fled"* (Mark 14:15).
3. They showed a vindictive spirit when the Samaritans would not receive them and refused to provide lodging for them, and James and John said, *"Lord, do you want us to command fire to come down from heaven and consume them, just as Elijah did? He turned and rebuked them and said, 'You don't know what manner of spirit you are of'"* (Mark 9:54-55).
4. Even Peter denied Him three times before he wept bitterly and was converted.

Jesus knew that if He was ever going to reach the world, these disciples needed to be sanctified (cleansed from the carnal element) and unified so that the world would believe that the Father had sent Him.

WHAT: Their Sanctity

Jesus prays, *"Sanctify them by Your truth. Your word is truth."* and *"And for their sakes I sanctify myself, that they also may be sanctified by the truth"* (John 17:17, 19).

The word sanctification has a dual meaning. It oftentimes means separation to God's use, and sometimes it means purification from moral defilement.

Separation to God's use is evidently the meaning in John 17:19, where Jesus says, *"For their sakes, I sanctify myself,"* for He was without sin (II Corinthians 5:21). He needed no sanctification in the sense of purification from sin. As human, though, He did need to set himself apart to be used by God the Father, especially by going to the cross for us.[28]

Jesus separated Himself to the death on the Cross in order that, *"He might sanctify and cleanse her* (the church) *with the washing of water by the word, that He might present her to Himself a glorious church, not having spot or wrinkle or any such thing, but that she should be holy and without blemish"* (Ephesians 5:26, 27). *"Therefore Jesus also, that He might sanctify the people with His own blood, suffered outside the gate"* (Hebrews 13:12).

When Jesus used the term **"sanctify"** of Himself, it was in the active voice: *"I sanctify myself."* Here is the objective meaning of sanctify: "I sanctify myself apart" to the death of the cross. When, however, the Lord spoke of the sanctification of the disciples, it was in the passive voice: "that they ... also may be sanctified." Here is something which the disciples could not do for themselves, but which must be done in and for them. The word "also" points to a moral dimension of the

---

28   J. Kenneth Grider, *A Wesleyan-Holiness Theology*, pg. 386

work of sanctification, giving reality to the image of Christ within (Romans 8:29; II Corinthians 3:18).[29]

In speaking of the sanctification of His disciples, Jesus meant the cleansing from the defilement of sin that came about through the fall of man. This is essential for communion with God and to be an effective servant of God.

In his first Epistle, John says, *"If we walk in the light as He is in the light, we have fellowship with one another, and the blood of Jesus Christ His Son cleanses us from all sin"* (I John 1:7). *"He who says he abides in Him ought himself also to walk just as He walked"* (I John 2:6). These two verses teach us what is required to walk and have fellowship with Him. We do not normally walk with someone with whom we share no common purpose. *"Can two walk together, unless they are agreed?"* (Amos 3:3). To walk after the flesh is to agree with the sinful propensities of our nature. However, when our nature is cleansed (sanctified), we walk not after the flesh, but we walk after and agree with the dictates of the Holy Spirit. We are sensitive to His sayings and obedient to His commands. But it is not a one-sided conversation, for He is interested in our concerns and burdens, as well. He asks us to *"cast all our care upon Him, for He cares for us"* (I Peter 5:7).

"Friendship with Jesus! Fellowship divine!
Oh, what blessed, sweet communion!
Jesus is a friend of mine.

"And He walks with me, and He talks with me,
And He tells me I am His own;
And the joy we share as we tarry there,
None other has ever known."

Paul, in Romans Chapter 6, admonished man was to *"present his members as slaves of righteousness for holiness."* In order to do that, he would have to be cleansed from the carnal mind. It is the

---

29   W. T. Purkiser, *Sanctification and its Synonyms,* Pg. 16

work of Sanctification that would resolve the problem of double-mindedness. If carnality remained within the heart, there would be a constant conflict within where the *flesh* would war against the Spirit. *"These are contrary to one another, so that you do not do the things that you wish"* (Galatians 5:17). The call to holiness is a call to harmony within oneself, as well as with God. We cannot serve efficiently or effectively as long as there is a dual allegiance within the heart. The heart being the fountain from which all of life flows, the fountain must be pure. Therefore, Paul says, *"The purpose of the commandment is love from a pure heart"* (I Timothy 1:5).

There are several elements that work together for the sanctification of the believer.

    a.   God is the originating cause of sanctification. (I Thessalonians 4:3).

    b.   Jesus is the provisional cause of sanctification. (Ephesians 5:25, 26).

    c.   Holy Spirit is the efficient cause of sanctification. (I Peter 1:2).

    d.   The Blood of Christ is the meritorious cause of sanctification. (Hebrews 13:12).

    e.   Faith is the conditional cause. (Acts 15:9).

When Jesus prayed, *"Sanctify them by your truth, your word is truth,"* we see according to Jesus, that "**truth**" is the instrumental cause of the believer's sanctification. This is stated in Verse 17 as well as Verse 19. What part does the Word have to play in our sanctification? We know that the psalmist said, *"Your **word** is a lamp to my feet and a light to my path"* (Psalms 119:105). Jesus stated a great truth while speaking concerning the branches (disciples) who were members of the true vine when He said, *"You are already clean because of the **word** which I have spoken to you"* (John 15:3). *"Christ also loved the church and gave Himself for her, that He might sanctify and cleanse her with the washing of water by the **word**"* (Ephesians 5:25-26).

The Word of God strikes deep into the heart exposing the depths of the remains of corruption and defilement therein, *"for the **word** of God is living and powerful, and sharper than any* *two-edged sword, piercing even to the division of soul and spirit, and of joints and marrow, and is a discerner of the thoughts and intents of the heart"* (Hebrews 4:12). When one comes to the Word with an open mind and a hungry heart, he will inevitably be brought into the light of entire sanctification. *"So then faith comes by hearing, and hearing by the **word** of God"* (Romans 10:17). There is an intrinsic power in the **Word** of God that generates faith. *"And the very God of peace Himself sanctify you completely,"* is followed by the triumphant promise, *"He who calls you is faithful, who also will do it"* (I Thessalonians 5:23-24). By faith in the living Word of God, we trust the cleansing blood of Christ and believe God to make it real. It is the word of truth which leads us to the knowledge of holiness, both as to our need and as to God's will for our lives.

WHY: Their Unity

"That they may be made perfect in one, and that the world may know that You have sent me, and have loved them as You have loved me," (John 17:23) that we be in a "oneness" with the triune Godhead. As God, the Father, the Son, and the Holy Spirit are co-equal and co-eternal, these three are one. There are certain skeptics and gainsayers who accuse the Christian of serving three gods in calculating the Trinity by addition. They say one, plus one, plus one equals three. However, if one would use multiplication rather than addition in their calculations, they would come nearer the truth. One Father, times one Son, times one Holy Spirit, and it comes out to one in unity. When you have one, you have the other two, and if you reject one, you reject the other two.

When we are sanctified wholly, there is a completeness in our oneness. *"For both He that sanctifies and those who are being sanctified are all of one, for which reason He is not ashamed to call them brethren"* (Hebrews 2:11). Look at the phrase, *"are all of one,"* perhaps it could read, *"are all 'out' of one."* My mother and father had twelve children, which obviously means that I have eleven siblings. Each of my eleven brothers and sisters can claim my parents as their own and be correct. When such a claim is made they take nothing from me, and I take nothing from them, because we all have, (*or are "all out of"*) the same parents. When one is born of the Spirit and receives the baptism of the Spirit, *"we are all of one; for which cause He is not ashamed to call us brethren."* Whatever may be our various human distinctions, idiosyncrasies, religious affiliations or anything else lose their significance. We are one, not in uniformity, but in unity with the Trinity.

When God made man and later said that it is not good that man be alone, *"He caused a deep sleep to fall on Adam, and he slept; and He took one of the ribs, and closed up the flesh in its place....and from the rib....He made into a woman....Adam said: This is now bone of my bone and flesh of my flesh; She shall be called woman, because she was taken out of man. Therefore a man shall leave his father and mother, and they shall become ONE flesh"* (Genesis 2:21-24).

Here we see an expression of oneness. C. S. Lewis understood the seriousness of the vows one takes at a wedding that makes the two become one and noted that when a married couple decides to divorce, it is more than the breaking of a contract; it is more like the severing of a limb from the body.

Christ likened the oneness of the husband and wife to Himself and the church. *"For we are members of His body, of His flesh and of His bones. For this reason a man shall leave his father and mother and be joined to his wife, and the two shall become one flesh. This is a great mystery, but I speak concerning Christ and the church"* (Ephesians 5:30-32).

Sanctification may be thought of as a word with one root and two shoots. Its root meaning is separation. From the root springs two shoots; one is dedication, which means separation to; the other is purification, which is separation from. The Christian dedicates; Christ purifies.[30]

It is like the branch that is in (at **one** with) the true vine. *"Every branch that bears fruit He prunes* (purges) *that it may bear more fruit."* It is this "**oneness in unity**," when all envy, strife, and divi-

---

30 Paul S. Rees, *Victorious and Fruitful Living*, Pg.114

sion has been purged away, that we are able to bring many sons and daughters into the kingdom. The fruit does not grow on the vine, but on the branches. If we prove faithful, one day we shall be with Him and behold His glory!

12

Jesus: The Lamb of God
(John 1:29-34)

The incarnation always had the cross of Calvary in its view. The cross was not an accident nor was it incidental; Jesus came on purpose for it. His death fulfills God's will for man's redemption. *"Therefore, when He came into the world, He said: 'Sacrifice and offering You did not desire, but a body You have prepared for me. In burnt offerings and sacrifices for sin You had no pleasure. Then I said, Behold, I have come—in the volume in the book it is written of Me—To do Your will, O God.'....then He said, 'Behold, I have come to do Your will, O God,' He takes away the first that He may establish the second. By the will we have been sanctified through the offering of the body of Jesus Christ once for all"* (Hebrews 10:5-7, 9-10).

In this passage we see that Jesus, as the Lamb of God, was the one and final sacrifice for the sin of the world. All previous sacrifices were the types that foreshadowed the one and only real sacrifice that was offered on Calvary's cross. Following the ignominious death on the cross, there was no longer any need for another sacrifice. All previous sacrifices could never *"make those who* (offered them) *approach perfect"* (Hebrews 10:1). In Hebrews 10:11 & 12, we notice that the earthly priests offered sacrifices repeatedly but because they never could take away sins they stood daily, but when Jesus, the Lamb of God, was offered Himself, it said following His resurrection He *"sat down* (work was completed) *at the Father's right hand."* By His death and resurrection, He fulfilled the demands of a broken law and became the propitiation for the sins of the whole world.

It has often been asked, "How could a loving God ever consign anyone to a place as horrible as hell?" The fact is God does not send one to hell; one just refuses to accept Him and heaven. The real question should be, seeing that all have sinned and fallen short of the glory of God, how is He able to keep from sending all of us to hell, and the answer is Calvary. The cross is the only effective ground upon which a sinner can approach God. When He died on the cross *"He made Him who knew no sin to be sin* (sin-offering) *for us, that we might become the righteousness of God in Him"* (II Corinthians 5:21).

C. H. Spurgeon:

He could destroy the sinner and punish him forever and remain just, but He would not be merciful as the Bible teaches Him to be. But if, on the other hand, He would forgive the sinner without pronouncing judgment on sin, He would create rouges galore. Christianity would be a mere sentimentalism, sinning would be of no consequence, and God would be nothing more than a benevolent Grandfather.

Therefore, justice and mercy embrace one another at the cross!

It was following His death, resurrection, and ascension that Jesus sent the Holy Spirit into the world as our "advocate." This is now the dispensation of the Holy Spirit, and He has come to perform various ministries. What Jesus provided on the cross of Calvary, He, as the executive of the Godhead, has come to make perpetually available and continuously operative in the hearts and lives of the Christian. Let us examine a few of the ministries that He has come to perform in this and other passages.

He is the great "revealer." Jesus said, *"when He is come, He will convict* (reprove, reveal, convince) *the world of sin"* (John 16:8). He brings to the soul a concious sense of the exceeding sinfulness of sin. He reveals that in the trespass of sin, man breaks the law of God but also He reveals that in the treason of sin, man betrays the love of God. He is faithful to reveal sin in all of its ugliness; Its disobedience, destruction, defilement, deformity, and depravity. He teaches us that Jesus came to save us from "ALL" sin.

He not only reproves man of sin, He is faithful to show us a way of escape from the wickedness and warp of sin, by revealing to us the Savior. In this passage we see the fulfillment of the words of Jesus when He said, *"He will not speak on His own authority, but whatever He hears He will speak; and He will tell you things to come. He will glorify Me, for He will take of what is Mine and declare it to you"* (John 16:13-14).

He Reveals His Peerless Person

Jesus is our pattern but there is no one His peer. He stands alone as the exclusive way, the infallible truth, and the eternal life. He is God's one and only Son, and He is the one and only acceptable sacrifice for the sin of the world. While the Holy Spirit reveals Jesus as our one and only Savior, Jesus reveals to us the Father. In response to Philip's request for Jesus to show him the Father, He said, *"He who has seen Me has seen the Father."*(John 14:9) God is known to us only in His Son, through the Holy Spirit, *"for through Him we both have access by one Spirit to the Father"* (Ephesians 2:18).

The Bible is Christ centered setting forth the mighty works of God provided by His Son. Through His death and resurrection He has provided for all lost men and women to be saved and filled with the Holy Spirit.

A.W. Tozer said,

> Everyone desires the fullness of the Holy Spirit but not the filling. They want the end result but not the means that produces it. It will require the abandonment of self to the leadership of the Holy Spirit and the Lordship of Christ.

The Holy Spirit reveals two things that the peerless person of Christ came to do. He came to be:

1. *"The Lamb of God that takes away the sin of the world"* (vs. 29).
2. *"This is He who baptizes with the Holy Spirit"* (vs. 33).

It is in these two verses that He reveals the way and by whom one's heart is cleansed from all sin. The way was provided by the sacrificial Lamb and administered by the Holy Spirit. God makes the redemptive sacrifice of the Savior a reality in the believer's heart and life by the gracious work of the Holy Spirit.

Whenever one experiences the baptism with the Holy Spirit, it may or may not be accompanied by an expression of emotion. One's emotional reactions vary from person to person. Regardless of the emotional content or lack thereof; that is not what is most important. What is most important is that He comes to cleanse and fill us with Himself and to assume total mastery over us and all we do thereafter.

As the *Lamb of God*, He came to deliver us from the *sin of the world*. He delivers us from individual sins, and He also cleanses us from inbred sin. This revelation of His peerless person left no room for doubt in John's mind concerning the Deity of our Lord; *"And I have seen and testified that this is the Son of God"* (John 1:34). The Lamb of God is our Liberator. We enter into spiritual life by the birth of the Spirit, and we are emancipated in life through the baptism of the Spirit. The Holy Spirit not only reproves of sin and reveals the Savior, through His baptism, He refines our soul.

He Reveals His Preferred Place

John the Baptist spoke three times concerning the fact that Jesus is more to be preferred than himself or anyone else. *"It is He who, coming after me, is preferred before me, whose sandal strap I am not worthy to loose"* (John 1:27). Three times John said that Jesus was preferred before him. (vs. 15, 27, 30) One day Jesus came to John to be baptized by him, and John tried to prevent Him, saying, *"I need to be baptized by You, and are You coming to me?"* (Matthew 3:14) The baptism that John was referring to was not the water baptism that he administered to those who had truly repented but the baptism with the Holy Ghost of which Christ alone could administer. Putting these two incidents together let us notice what this teaches us. Remember, John the Baptist made these two confessions; *"I need to be baptized by You"* and Jesus is *"preferred before me."*

Therefore, these confessions were made by one of the greatest men the world has ever known. Jesus said, *"Among those born of women there has not risen one greater than John the Baptist"* (Mat-

91

thew 11:11). John said he was a God-sent man (John 1:6). He was the fore-runner of Christ, preparing the way for the Lord. He preached the whole counsel of God. He was so true to his mission that he rebuked rulers in their sin even though it meant that he would be be-headed. He was devoid of all unholy ambition, for he encouraged his disciples to follow Jesus and said, *"He must increase and I must decrease."*

There were those who thought that he was the Messiah. John said, *"I'm not the Christ, I am the voice of one crying in the wilderness: make straight the way of the Lord"* (John 1:20, 23). He was just the **"Voice,"** Jesus was the authority behind the voice, the Master of the man, the might in the message, sovereign over his soul. He the Son of God is preferred before the saved.

As John taught and lived that Jesus must hold favor, pre-eminence, and preference over him, it is certainly true of everyone else that comes after Him. The struggle that goes on at an altar is certainly not a struggle with God, but it is the soul's struggling to rid itself of anything and everything that wants to hold the place of preferment which rightfully belongs to Christ. This is the reason, following conversion or the birth of the Spirit, one must seek the baptism of the Holy Spirit for cleansing from the remains of carnality in the heart. *"Because the carnal mind is enmity against God; for it is not subject to the law of God, nor indeed can be"* (Romans 8:7). The carnal mind will never consent to giving Him the preferred place in the heart, and Jesus will not long remain where His Lordship is challenged.

If carnality is not cleansed from the heart by the Baptism with the Holy Spirit, it will soon generate a dislike for holiness. This carnal mind manifests itself in a spirit of self-centeredness, self-defensiveness, self-sparing, and self-justification and will not die easily. Its nature is always repulsive of truth, holiness, and righteousness but always gravitates toward error and its bent is always in the direction of evil.

He Reveals His Promised Provisions

John the Baptist preached, *"Repent, for the kingdom of heaven is at hand!"* Many from all over the region who came to hear him were taken by his ministry and *"were baptized by him in the Jordan, confessing their sins."* When the Pharisees and Sadducees came to his baptism, *"he said to them, 'Brood of vipers! Who warned you to flee from the wrath to come? Therefore bear fruits worthy of repentance"* (Matthew 3:2-8).

John demanded that all who received his baptism had to give evidence that they had confessed and repented of all their sins and renounced their old life. He told them that they could not rely on their rich Hebrew heritage to save them for he said, *"God is able to raise up children to Abraham from these stones."* He then makes a prophetic announcement when he said, *"And even now the ax is laid to the root of the trees. Therefore every tree which does not bear good fruit is cut down and thrown into the fire. 'I indeed baptize you with water unto repentance, but He who is coming after me is mightier than I, whose sandals I am not worthy to carry. He will baptize you with the Holy Spirit and fire. His winnowing fan is in His hand, and He will thoroughly clean out His threshing floor, and gather His wheat into the barn; but He will burn up the chaff with unquenchable fire"* (Matthew 3:9-12).

Following His resurrection and before He ascended back to the Father's right hand, Jesus gave this command to His disciples, *"Do not depart from Jerusalem, but wait for the promise of the Father, which, He said, you have heard of me. For John truly baptized with water, but you shall be baptized with the Holy Spirit not many days from now"* (Acts 1:4-5). What John prophesied, Jesus provided by His death and resurrection and was now the promise of the soon to be ascended Christ.

We must recognize that there are two distinct baptisms being referenced here by Jesus. Each of these ministries had their distinct purpose. John's baptism was to signify that the sinner had truly repented and been converted. Jesus' baptism was in response to the believer's presentation of himself and total consecration to the whole will of God. John used water, a very impersonal agent, to officiate his baptism, and it was poured out upon the skin. Jesus used the Holy Spirit, a very personal agent, to administer His baptism, and instead of it being outward (on the skin) as John's was, it was inward, in the spirit.

While John the Baptist could perform the ceremonial baptism of water, he could not perform the baptism with the Holy Spirit. As any God-called minister can administer water baptism, none can administer the baptism with the Holy Spirit. This is an exclusive ministry that only Jesus can administer because, as John the Baptist stated, He alone is *mighty* and *worthy* enough to baptize with the Holy Spirit.

This experience of the baptism with the Holy Spirit involves the possession of someone else, Christ! Everything carnal and selfish is burned out with the Holy Spirit's fire. It consumes the dross and purifies all that remains. It is recorded that on the Day of Pentecost, *"There appeared to them divided tongues, as of fire, and one sat upon each of them. And they were all filled with the Holy Spirit and began to speak with other tongues, as the Spirit gave them utterance."*

Carlyle said that the spread of the Faith in its earliest days had little or nothing to do with external organization. "How did Christianity arise and spread among men? Was it by institutions, and establishments, and mechanical systems? No! It arose in the mystic deeps of a man's soul, and was spread by simple, altogether natural, and individual efforts. It flew like hallowed fire from heart to heart till all were purified and illumined by it." [31]

The church of the 21st century is in desperate need of the baptism with the Holy Spirit and fire. If the Acts of the Apostles is a true account of the early church, (and I do not say that as though I do not believe it is the true account of the early church) it is obvious and we must conclude that the church today is living far below its privileges. While Acts chapter 2 reveals the inaugural Day of Pentecost

---

31   Joe Brice, *Pentecost*, Pgs. 70-71

and much cannot be repeated, the spirit of Pentecost can and must be perpetuated. In the Spirit's fullness, the church finds the power of expression and execution for the task He has called her to perform. In J. B. Phillips preface to his book entitled, *The Young Church in Action, a Translation of the Acts of the Apostles*, he writes:

> This surely is the church as it was meant to be. It is vigorous and flexible, for these are the days before it ever became fat and short of breath through prosperity, or musclebound by overorganization. These men did not make "acts of faith," they believed; they did not "say their prayers," they really prayed. They did not hold conferences on psychosomatic medicine, they simply healed the sick. ... No one can read this book without being convinced that there is Someone here at work besides mere human beings.

13

Holiness: Its Beauty and Mystery
(Colossians 1:26-29)

For nearly 52 years I have been enjoying blessed communion with my Lord and Savior and sweet fellowship with His children. I am grateful that the first exposure that I ever had for Christ was in a church that believed and practiced a life of love (*agape*). I am most thankful for a pastor who faithfully proclaimed the doctrine of "second blessing holiness," a phrase that many quibble over, but to me, the phrase is sweeter than honey. Early in my Christian walk I was taught that *"He is also able to save to the uttermost those who come to God through Him, since He always lives to make intercession for them"* (Hebrews 7:25). It was four weeks following my conversion that I began to experience the chastening of the Lord. His chastening is the way He leads His obedient children to partake of His holiness. If one does not receive His chastening, *"then you are illegitimate and not sons"* (Hebrews 12:5-10). Two things are evident by His chastening, one is that it is a sign that He loves them and secondly that they are truly His children. Through the faithful preaching of His word and the loving chastening of my Lord, I entered into this beautiful relationship with my Lord. In 52 years, I have never found Him lacking or insufficient for any need that I have had in my life. Since the day that I received Him as my Savior, it has been my high privilege to worship Him in the beauty of holiness.

Holiness is beautiful in all realms. Like a diamond it has many facets to it, and they all sparkle with luminous glory. Holiness is beautiful in spite of its enemies' efforts to misrepresent it. Holiness is also beautiful in spite of its friends who unwittingly misuse it. "A jewel is still a jewel, however incrusted in base alloys. The alloys

96

may hide the precious gem or disfigure its beauty, but cannot destroy its value. It is the task of Christian patience to remove the debasing incrustations and set it in position."[32]

The beauty of holiness is that it is a life of love. The love that would reach out to an unloving people, of which I was one, and even though we were enemies of the cross of Christ, He died for us. His life exemplified what He taught when He said: *"Love your enemies, bless those who curse you, do good to those who hate you, and pray for those who spitefully use you and persecute you"* (Matthew 5:44). It is this same love that He imparts to His children in regeneration, is made perfect in entire sanctification, and abounds more and more as we walk in the light with Him. The one and only law that is essential and comprehensive is the law of love. When asked by the lawyer, *"Teacher, which is the great commandment in the law?" Jesus said to him, "Ye shall love the Lord your God with all your heart, with all your soul, and with all your mind. This is the first and great commandment. And the second is like it: You shall love your neighbor as yourself"* (Matthew 22:36-39).

There are those who oppose this great Biblical doctrine because of **ignorance**. That is why it is incumbent upon every preacher to proclaim this truth scripturally, persistently, and lovingly. There are many voices that would try to give alternatives to holiness as a second definite work of grace, whereby the heart is cleansed from sin. For example:

1. There are those who say that as long as we are in the body we will never be free from sin. We will have to suppress "our old man" and his works. The word "old" refers to its antiquity because it has been in existence since Adam's fall. The word "our" shows how personal it is because all mankind has inherited this nature through Adam (Romans 5:12). However, the word teaches us that, *"our old man was crucified with Him, that the body of sin might be done away with, that we should no longer be slaves of sin"* (Romans 6:6).

---

32   Roy S. Nicholson, *True Holiness*, pg. 21

97

2. Another theory is that entire sanctification comes by a long and never complete process of growth. We admit that there is growth in grace previous to and following the work of entire sanctification, but we strongly disagree that anyone could ever grow into this work of grace that is received by faith. *"Now the God of peace Himself sanctify you completely, and may your whole spirit, and soul, and body be preserved blameless at the coming of our Lord Jesus Christ. He who calls you is faithful, who also will do it"* (I Thessalonians 5:23-24). Those who teach the growth theory are confusing purity with maturity.

3. There are those who teach that one is sanctified through and through at the point of death. That makes death their sanctifier rather than the blood of Christ.

4. There are others who teach that one will go through purgatory after death and finally qualify for heaven. There have never been any witnesses who pose these theories that could testify in this life to a clean heart.

The scripture in Hebrews 12:14 tells us that holiness is the condition for one to see the Lord. The writer says, *"without which* (holiness) *no one will see the Lord."* It is the negative way of saying what Jesus said positively in the Sermon on the Mount, *"Blessed are the pure in heart, for they shall see God"* (Matthew 5:8). There are various other substitutes for this experience, but none of them will enable one to fulfill God's will and command. He has admonished the Christian to *"put on the new man which was created according to God, in true righteousness and holiness"* (Ephesians 4:24).

There are others who reject this truth out of **prejudice** because some who have testified to this work of grace in their life did not demonstrate it in their conduct. Their pious talk was not complemented by their practical walk. I would remind the reader that in spite of the fact that this holy experience may be brought into disrepute by inconsistent and abusive professors, it does not change the truth. It is important that we who have experienced this work of grace keep in mind that the world cannot see Christ crowned within, but they will measure us by the Christian conduct without. Let us persuade them by a consistent demonstration of the life of holiness.

There are still those who reject it because of **unbelief**. It will require the Holy Spirit to enlighten and bring conviction to the need of this experience upon the heart of the genuine believer. He alone can uncover the evil heart of unbelief. On the part of the believer who is the recipient of Holy Spirit's conviction, he has to show a hunger and thirst for righteousness in order to be filled. Confession of his need will be the first step, in spite of all of his prejudice and unbelief. Confess simply means, *"to agree with."* One must take sides against himself and all other skeptics and agree with the truth as it is in Christ. He must silence all other voices and believe not only that the experience is possible but that God is able to fully satisfy the need of the soul. Finally he must make a total consecration of all he is and has to God, and by faith appropriate the provisions of Calvary.

> The greatest problem in the universe is the sin problem. The happiest fact in the universe is that God has a solution to the sin problem. The heart-rending fact is that the overwhelming majority of the world's people reject God's solution to the sin problem. Salvation is wholeness, soundness, cleanness, in a word, "holiness."
>
> The smallest minority of the world's population is composed of those who wholly and forever are devoted to the will of God. His will is the supreme rule of their lives. There is another—and larger—minority group who are no doubt believers in Jesus Christ, yet they are "double minded" (James 1:8). They have not wholly committed themselves to the complete will of God for their lives. But the vast majority of the world's peoples have abandoned themselves to sin. They live without any regard for the will of God. Their pattern of life is carnal—self versus God. This carnality is referred to by various terms and figurative language. But it is that nature or disposition out of which sinful acts spring. It is "the sin" from which Jesus came into the world to save man (Read John 1:29; I John 1:7-9) [33]

---

33 Roy S. Nicolson, "The Supreme Hostility to Holiness," *God's Revivalist*, November 5, 1981

Remember that only two out of the 12 spies who went in to spy out the land of Canaan came back excited about what they had seen and even brought back fruit as evidence. Caleb and Joshua wanted to go up and possess the land (and were later allowed to enter Canaan), but the majority refused and they never entered into the promised rest of Canaan. *"Therefore, since a promise remains of entering His rest, let us fear lest any of you should seem to come short of it. ... There remains therefore a rest for the people of God"* (Hebrews 4:1, 9).

The Apostle Paul says, *"The mystery which has been hidden from ages and from generations, but now has been revealed to His saints. To them God willed to make known what are the riches of the glory of this mystery among the Gentiles: which is Christ in you, the hope of glory. Him we preach, warning every man and teaching every man in all wisdom, that we may present every man perfect in Christ Jesus. To this end I also labor, striving according to His working which works in me mightily"* (Colossians 1:26-29).

It was for this purpose, *to present every man perfect in Christ Jesus*, that the Apostle was willing to suffer the loss of all things. This "perfection" is the necessary requirement for the enthronement of Christ in the hearts of men which would be the hope of eternal glory. This coronation of Christ in the heart is the very essence of holiness and the eternal hope of the saint.

Holiness is Reasonable

In Paul's use of the word **mystery**, he is stating a truth that there are some things known only through divine revelation. Paul says in another letter, *"Eye has not seen, nor ear heard, nor have entered into the heart of man the things which God has prepared for those who love Him. **But God has revealed them to us through His Spirit.** For the Spirit searches all things, yes, the deep things of God."* While holiness seems to be a mystery to so many, it is most reasonable to those who have entered into it by faith.

There is nothing irrational about the holiness message even though much of it transcends human reasoning. The great verities of the Christian faith do not always lend themselves to the definition of the finite mind. There is something miraculous and mysterious about the new birth and sanctification, but it can become a reality in Christian experience and an enjoyment in life through faith. One stated that any religion that is not too big for the head is too small for the heart. What we may not be able to comprehend with our head, we can by faith appropriate in our heart.

Holiness is Desirable

Modern man is very concerned about his health and welfare in this world. We insist on having pure water and having our food inspected lest we be contaminated with bacteria that might cause typhoid or other deadly diseases. We go at great length and expense to have pure air to breathe. We work hard to keep our homes clean, our eating utensils sterile, and our clothes laundered. If one receives an injury the first thing we do is wash the wound and put a disinfectant on it so we will not contract an infection. All of this and much more is not only necessary but very desirable.

If we desire health for our bodies, sanity for our minds, cleanliness for our environment, then we should desire holiness for the soul. Holiness is the only standard that conditions us for fellowship with our holy Savior. It is only with a holy heart and righteous life that we will become a pleasure to our Lord. As true measurement is desirable to the scientist, truth is desirable to the philosopher, color is desirable to the artist, true tone is desirable to the musician, holiness is most desirable to the Christian.

At least four times the psalmist speaks of the "beauty" of holiness. Sin is the antithesis of holiness, and is very ugly. If one doesn't want holiness then they want sin. When I personally recognized sin's defilement and the remains of depravity in my heart following my conversion, I did not want to believe that I had to continuously suppress this nature. I believed that God who died to forgive me of the guilt of my sins, also could cleanse me from the remains of sin within. I certainly did not want to think that His blood was not efficacious (effective) enough to cleanse me from all sin. The same Spirit that brought Jesus from the dead, has power enough, through

His baptism, to cleanse me from all depravity. Praise the Lord! It is most desirable.

Holiness is Indispensable

The Bible makes it very clear that to be made holy is the only way to heaven. *"Blessed are the pure in heart, for they shall see God"* (Matthew 5:8). *"Pursue peace with all people, and holiness, without which no one will see the Lord"* (Hebrews 12:14). The necessity of holiness is an inherent necessity, because it is written in the moral order of things. God who is holy could not but require holiness as the standard for man. Man is the only creature that has been given the power of choice and therefore the only creature capable of holiness.

We respect the "without whiches" of all other areas of our lives. If we are going to fly on an airplane we must have a ticket, "without which" we will not board the plane. We must have a passport, sometimes a visa, and often times vaccinations and inoculations in order to enter some countries, "without which" we will not gain entrance. We never argue or dispute with these requirements; we just comply. We know that these are sovereign nations that have the right and the power to declare the terms by which we will arrive on their soil.[34]

God is Sovereign of heaven and earth and has every right to declare the terms and requirements necessary for us to spend eternity in His presence. He has made it perfectly clear that "holiness of heart and life" is His standard. We cannot reject holiness without, at the same time, rejecting Him and heaven. *"For this is the will of God, your sanctification....He who rejects this does not reject man, but God, who has also given us His Holy Spirit"* (I Thessalonians 4:3, 8). A person's desire for heaven cannot be greater than their desire for holiness. If there is no desire to be holy down here, one would be unfit for heaven over there.

---

34 Richard S. Taylor, Sermon

Holiness is Available

God never requires of one what He does not make available the provisions to meet that requirement. We must never talk about the availability of holiness except in relation to the cross. If we do we will end up with a humanistic approximation toward holiness rather than an experiential realization through the blood of the cross. *"Therefore Jesus also, that He might sanctify the people with His own blood, suffered outside the gate. Therefore let us go forth to Him, outside the camp, bearing His reproach. For here we have no continuing city, but we seek the one to come"* (Hebrews 12:12, 13). We can no more experience Christian perfection by growth than we can save ourselves by good works. It is all available through the blood of the cross.

"Christ in you, the hope of glory," is the mystery that is revealed. There are three classes in the New Testament with respect to hope:

1. *"Having no hope and without God in the world"* (Ephesians, 2:12). They are lost and make no profession of faith.

2. There is a class of people who have a false hope, and coming to the day of judgment, will say, *"Lord, Lord, have we not prophesied in Your name, cast our demons in Your name, and done many wonders in Your name? And then I will declare to them, I never knew you; depart from me, you who practice lawlessness"* (Matthew 7:22, 23).

3. The third class have experienced the truth of the text and have Christ enthroned within. That is the hope which is *"sure and steadfast, and which enters the Presence behind the veil"* (Hebrews 6:19). Our only hope is the enthronement of Christ within the holy of holies in the heart.

My hope is built on nothing less
Than Jesus' blood and righteousness
I dare not trust the sweetest frame,
But wholly lean on Jesus' name.